NEW IRISH POETS

NEW
IRISH POETS

REPRESENTATIVE SELECTIONS FROM
THE WORK OF 37 CONTEMPORARIES

Edited by Devin A. Garrity *(no date)*

with woodcuts by Harry Kernoff, R.H.A.   *242*

THE DEVIN-ADAIR COMPANY
NEW YORK: 1948

Printed in U.S.A.

typography by Peter Döblin

Ireland has always had more than her share of poets: today the number of those practicing the craft is greater than ever. But partly due to the recent war and partly because a few giants have tended to dominate the field in the minds of the public, the emergence of a new group of talented Irish contemporaries has managed to remain a virtual secret outside the British Isles.

In 1947 some of these poets of contemporary Ireland were first called to our attention with the publication of Kathleen Hoagland's 1000 YEARS OF IRISH POETRY, where a dozen or more were represented. The present volume is an attempt to survey the entire field and to introduce some of the best of this new talent to American lovers of poetry.

With a single exception then, the poets in this anthology are new to America. Some are youngsters just out of their teens; others have been around a long time, known and recognized at home but completely unknown outside. Only Austin Clarke has been published briefly in book form in the U.S.A., and this earlier work of his failed to receive the attention it might have had.

Other modern Irish poets who might be expected to be present if they had not already received American recognition in book form are: C. Day Lewis, published by Oxford and Louis Mac-Neice published by Random House, both widely available; Robert Farren, published by Sheed & Ward; W. R. Rodgers, published by Harcourt, Brace; Denis Devlin, published by Reynal & Hitchcock; Thomas McGreevy, published by Viking, and Patrick Kavanagh, published by Macmillan. Any comprehensive study of contemporary Irish poetry must include the work of these seven living poets —and the translations of Frank O'Connor. An effort to hold the present volume down to reasonable size would have necessitated their exclusion here under any circumstance.

An anthology is arbitrary at best; the present selection consists of poems that have given enjoyment to the editor. No apology is made for anything—or anyone—included or excluded, but an effort has been made to strike a balance, to provide fare for varied tastes and as much originality as possible.

Using the poetry itself as a guide, one will find it difficult indeed
to determine the political or religious leanings of the poets. This in
a land so often defined rigidly in terms of sectarian Protestantism
and sectarian Catholicism should come as a surprise to most Americans. Even more noteworthy perhaps is the presence of two Jewish
poets. If a scarcity of religious poems be noted it reflects the dearth
of good religious poetry being written today in one of the most
religious countries of the West.

Typifying present day Ireland the thirty-seven contributors come
from all sorts of backgrounds. The political left and the political
right are here. The Anglo-Irish, the Orangeman and the several
Gaels are present, and so are the city-worker and the farmer, the
university professor and the lighthouse keeper. The photographic
section at the back should provide the anthropologically minded
with interesting material.

A great many of the poems first appeared in the pages of *The
Dublin Magazine, The Bell,* and *The Irish Times.* These three
periodicals in particular deserve credit for the encouragement they
have given to poets and poetry in Ireland. Other poems were first
published in *The Irish Press, The Irish Bookman* and *The Capuchin
Annual.* A number were taken from the published volumes of the
poets, and still others are published here for the first time.

The editor is indebted to Valentin Iremonger for many sugges-
tions and for his generally constructive criticism, and to Leslie
Daiken, who provided the initial impetus for this book and who is
responsible for the inclusion of a number of its best poems.

D.A.G.

CONTENTS

HUGH CONNELL

MAURICE JAMES CRAIG

LESLIE DAIKEN

LYLE DONAGHY

PADRAIC FALLON

PADRAIC FIACC

MONK GIBBON

ROBERT GREACEN

SAM HARRISON

GEORGE HETHERINGTON

JOHN HEWITT

VALENTIN IREMONGER

SEÁN JENNETT

D. L. KELLEHER

FREDA LAUGHTON

ETHNA MacCARTHY

DONAGH MacDONAGH

PATRICK MacDONOGH

ROY McFADDEN

PATRICK MAYBIN

W. B. STANFORD

PATRIC STEVENSON

FRANCIS STUART

GEOFFREY TAYLOR

BRUCE WILLIAMSON

DENIS WRAFTER

LAND-FALL

Mariner, in the green spire
In the cold shell
Of the weaving sea,
What did you hear
As the mast and the sun went under,
The faint shore singing
Through your water-logged ear?
The lost crew ringing
A bell in the swirl of their doom?
As your vessel foundered
Went down in the ocean's thunder
To a world without sound
A world without end, Amen.

Luckless you were in your last land-fall,
O, Mariner,
Luckless to hear not children calling
You home to the green shore,
The harbour's calm,
Stone walls
And brown nets drying in the wind,
But the water tolling over
Spume and flurry, wreck and pebble,
Telling your breath's end
In a bubble's
Silence.
Luckless your homecoming
After long searching for the sandy inlet
Where we found you, trailing wrack,
A stranger naked at our creaking door.

Into the land of exile
This our exile
This your last port of call.

17

Spring sunlight strokes and warms
The headlands basking lazily
Like whales, and the gull glides
Overhead, angel-white
This morning, the sea's sole witness,
Come from the grave-digging storm
As the first stone thuds on the unnamed wood.

Lie easy, Mariner,
O, prodigal, for whom no calf was fattened.
Not the green waves' elegy
Do you hear in the dark clay,
But our only tribute, grief
For an unclaimed stranger, the tears of those
Who live between the breaking and the broken leaf.

THE DAY

Time holds no purring hour-glass to your face;
Its hounds, called off the hunt, lope past this cove,
This green and hedgy ledge of noon Time's grace
Allows us. Across the sailing bay you gaze,
Your eyes sky-coloured by the haloed view
Of islands. Time is away this day, my love.

Fuchsia bells swing soundlessly, the tide,
Feathering oars, wrinkles the rock-pool where
A cloud floats, the minutes at anchor ride.
This is your heart's high noon, my love, its hey-day
Here and now, the glittering view, the brief
Music, the song of the sun in your hair.

Time is away, but late or soon the tide
Must change direction. Come then, my love,
While light still flashes like a dolphin on the bay,
Let us explore, before the clock hands move,
This dangled day, the fabulous country
That lies between us and futurity.

CARAVANS—DUBLIN

OLD MICHAEL

Having scrubbed away the gray sweat
Of his last, this his least hurried death,
The hired woman lowers the blinds
In the small room of his quenched breath
On him who lies there, penny-eyed.

Outside, along the whitewashed wall
His flowers turn to the climbing light
And the cock that crew his hour nods sleepily
In the corner where old Michael used to sit
Smoking his evening pipe, in argument.

Now in the village of his origin
His praises are shared out among
The living voices, and the living speak
In parables of him whose hands
Could break a stallion or graft a rose.

Now in the lank and weeping grasses
Of the graveyard where his kith and kin await
His coming, between the mossy
Angels and the leaning crosses
His grave lies open to the spelling light.

And here tomorrow they will lay old Michael,
Whose yellow hands in sculptured peace are set,
Deep in the clay that was his cruellest lover,
His clay to nourish yet the longing root
Of the wild daffodil, the ivy leaf.

THE GARDEN

Fruit breaks on the summer mouth.
Between the frail leaf and the swaying light
Fair weather holds, and there is laughter in the grass—

Laughter and lovers arms and eyes as bright
As the water glancing at the anchored sky.

But do not cross too soon
The doorway through the high green wall.
Once entered, it is impossible from there to see
The ships that sail out of the shallow bay
After the harvest, the fruit fall, before the frost.

It is not clear immediately why
The birds that seemed content fly suddenly southwards,
Darkening for an hour the easy air,
For in this enclosed season of the heart
Beneath the boughs of summer and desire,
Who heeds or hears the bony wings of famine,
Or sees the eagles gathering, the farms afire?

THE HOSTS

Who shall welcome home
The soldier or the gray
Exile from shelterless seas?
Who shall hold out hands
To the late arrivals
Stumbling without a light?
Who shall hold the keys
To this shuttered house,
You, the ghost, or I, the living man?

For the days are short, the hours
Numbered upon the clock,
The guests will soon arrive,
The honoured one be back;
But who will stand within
The deep shadow of this door;
Who will light the lamps,
Dust of the hidden air,
You, the ghost, or I, the living man?

THE SETTLED MEN

No sly usurping dream defeats the will
Of these whose kingdoms are their careful crops.
Only the unwatched weeds breed loss,
Only the thoughtless sky contests
Against the slow resourcefulness of these
Who move between bare weathering headlands,
Moving until the stubborn heart is stayed.

Gravely, as gravely they live as the stones
That wall about their season-worried fields.
When death's encroaching wind unsettles hold
One falls, one stone, one man whose loss
Opens a door of prayer on every hearth.
Then without hesitancy or fear
Another thrusts into the vacant place.

Across their skies the sun leans sometimes or
The tall rain swings. The white day like a blade
Slips into night's sheath gradually, night
That nurses no sprouting fantasies of wealth,
But stretches a shadow on the marriage bed,
And in its darkness breeds the hands,
The hands of future toil and later ghosts.

Within their boundaries of clutching field
They are the uncommuning men. Absent
Is History, busy with war and loss.
Above them loneliness circles like a bird.
Beneath their silences the hard land yields.
Tall on Time's hill, they breathe the plucking air,
These men who through the centuries grew gaunt.

ONE KINGFISHER
AND ONE YELLOW ROSE

Taking pity on this scrag-end of the city
Is my one kingfisher
Sitting stiffly on his willow
And staring at my one yellow rose.
I like him for his blueness
And more so for his kindness,
But I wish I had a garden
Then I wouldn't be depending
On this one kingfisher
And on one yellow rose.

There's a man, says one who knows,
Who is always in a hurry—
His mind's on making money
For a garden
Where he harbours
Many a kingly fisher
And many a quality rose.
But he's not the man he was,
Says my one who knows,
Since his fellows stopped saluting him
With: How's your one kingfisher?
And: How's that yellow rose?

MAY EVENING

A water hen is hopping
through the shade of twenty greens
of twenty trees
in this heart of Dublin
and a silenced newsboy listens

to the rain wet blackbird,
lets his nose get in the water
to keep eye with the dipping back,
red beak,
of the water hen;
he broods on the blue tits
and the nesting swan
until all his custom
on the nearby street
is gone.

EVENING ON HOWTH HEAD

Whee hee lo, whee hee . . . .
Wood pigeons—gentle as the wind
sleeping
as the sky
deepening
more than sea.

Sad as the waves coming
rarily
and the mist moving
mountainy
in from the sea.

Wood sounds
eternally
move the goats
drowsily
into the cyclamen
arms of the sea.

FIRST WOMAN'S LAMENT

My man is a bone ringèd with weed.

    Thus it was on my bridal night;
    That the sea, risen to a green wall
    At our window; quenching love's new delight,
    Stood curved between me and the midnight call
    Of him who said I was so fair
    He could drown for joy in the salt of my hair.
        We sail, he said,
        Like the placid dead
        That have long forgotten the marriage-bed.

    On my bridal-night
    Brine stung the window.
    Alas, in every night since then
    These eyes have rained
    For him who made my heart sing
    At the lifting of the latch;
    For him who will not come again
    Weary from the sea.

The wave tore his bright flesh in her greed:
My man is a bone ringèd with weed.

SECOND WOMAN'S LAMENT

He was not only friend and my lover,
But as a centaur is united and divided in one creature
So he between the bursting of white seas
Was man and craft together
But on shore was neither.

Fearful of fear: of death-encounter missed,
At night he was pho'rescent,
Gleamed blue fire in flying darkness,
Shone with fishscales as he stared
Naked, at the window-rush of storm
And spume, the death of waves.
And O my God, the pain beneath my bones
At the grinding of shells and stone;
The gnawing-away of my sweet patch of earth
Held jealously from the tide, that my children
May touch grass and flowers;
Turning from the whale's way and flying fish
To plough their furrow in the firm-set land.

But he was salt, and very rib of his boat;
Aching to plunge an oar into black night,
And throw his challenge out in lanes of light.

SONG

Heron is harsh with despair
For the felled pine of the upland:
Curlew is torn in her love
For the sea and the hill.
Heart in my breast is a stone
That my man cannot hold me
When hawthorn and plum are
Brave with the blossom of Spring.

GIVE NO WHITE FLOWER

If the woman in the purple petticoat
Thinks that you love her,
Take her a handful of mosses
And an offering of yellow asphodel.
Give no white flower

ROWING A CURRAGH—CONNEMARA

I would not have her heart broken by you:
Her heart torn open
You would see the intricate plan of it,
The valves of exquisite shape,
The cusp,
The veins running over the surface.
And if you watched
The ordered beat of blood would thicken,
Stifling her to quick death.
Then there would be no more
A woman standing with expectant hands
When the tide falls away from the shore.

SONG

Bone-aged is my white horse;
Blunted is the share;
Broken the man who through sad land
Broods on the plough.

Bone-bright was my gelding once;
Burnished was the blade;
Beautiful the youth who in green Spring
Broke earth with song.

NIGHT AND MORNING

I know the injured pride of sleep,
The strippers at the mocking-post,
The insult in the house of Caesar
And every moment that can hold
In brief the miserable act
Of centuries. Thought can but share
Belief—and the tormented soul,
Changing confession to despair,
Must wear a borrowed robe.

Morning has moved the dreadful candle,
Appointed shadows cross the nave;
Unlocked by the secular hand,
The very elements remain
Appearances upon the altar.
Adoring priest has turned his back
Of gold upon the congregation.
All saints have had their day at last,
But thought still lives in pain.

How many councils and decrees
Have perished in the simple prayer
That gave obedience to the knee;
Trampling of rostrum, feathering
Of pens at cock-rise, sum of reason
To elevate a common soul:
Forgotten as the minds that bled
For us, the miracle that raised
A language from the dead.

O when all Europe was astir
With echo of learned controversy,
The voice of logic led the choir.

Such quality was in all being,
The forks of heaven and this earth
Had met, town-walled, in mortal view
And in the pride that we ignore,
The holy rage of argument,
God was made man once more.

TENEBRAE

This is the hour that we must mourn
With tallows on the black triangle,
Night has a napkin deep in fold
To keep the cup; yet who dare pray
If all in reason should be lost,
The agony of man betrayed
At every station of the cross?

O when the forehead is too young,
Those centuries of mortal anguish,
Dabbed by a consecrated thumb
That crumbles into dust, will bring
Despair with all that we can know;
And there is nothing left to sing,
Remembering our innocence.

I hammer on that common door,
Too frantic in my superstition,
Transfix with nails that I have broken,
The angry notice of the mind.
Close as the thought that suffers him,
The habit every man in time
Must wear beneath his ironed shirt.

An open mind disturbs the soul,
And in disdain I turn my back
Upon the sun that makes a show

Of half the world, yet still deny
The pain that lives within the past,
The flame sinking upon the spike,
Darkness that man must dread at last.

THE LUCKY COIN

Collect the silver on a Sunday,
Weigh the pennies of the poor,
His soul can make a man afraid
And yet thought will endure.
But who can find by any chance
A coin of different shape
That never came from Salamanca
Or danced on chapel plate?

Though time is slipping through all fingers
And body dare not stay,
That lucky coin, I heard men tell it,
Had glittered once in Galway
And crowds were elbowing the spirit
While every counter shone,
Forgetting grief until the ages
Had changed it for a song.

Turning in cartwheels on the fairground,
The sun was hastier—
That strolling girls might have for dowry,
Two hands about a waist;
Men voted for the Liberator
After the booths were closed
And only those in failing health
Remembered their own souls.

On Nephin many a knot was tied,
The sweet in tongue made free there,
Lovers forgot on the mountain-side

The stern law of the clergy
That kiss, pinch, squeeze, hug, smack denied,
Forgot the evil, harm
And scandal that come closer, lying
In one another's arms.

Not one of us will ever find
That coin of different shape
For it was lost before our rising
Or stolen—as some say.
But when our dread of the unseen
Has rifled hole and corner,
How shall we praise the men that freed us
From everything but thought.

THE STRAYING STUDENT

On a holy day when sails were blowing southward,
A bishop sang the Mass at Inishmore,
Men took one side, their wives were on the other
But I heard the woman coming from the shore:
And wild in despair my parents cried aloud
For they saw the vision draw me to the doorway.

Long had she lived in Rome when Popes were bad,
The wealth of every age she makes her own,
Yet smiled on me in eager admiration,
And for a summer taught me all I know,
Banishing shame with her great laugh that rang
As if a pillar caught it back alone.

I learned the prouder counsel of her throat,
My mind was growing bold as light in Greece;
And when in sleep her stirring limbs were shown,
I blessed the noonday rock that knew no tree:
And for an hour the mountain was her throne,
Although her eyes were bright with mockery.

They say I was sent back from Salamanca
And failed in logic, but I wrote her praise
Nine times upon a college wall in France.
She laid her hand at darkfall on my page
That I might read the heavens in a glance
And I knew every star the Moors have named.

Awake or in my sleep, I have no peace now,
Before the ball is struck, my breath has gone,
And yet I tremble lest she may deceive me
And leave me in this land, where every woman's son
Must carry his own coffin and believe,
In dread, all that the clergy teach the young.

THE BLACKBIRD OF DERRYCAIRN
(*from the Irish*)

Stop, stop and listen for the bough top
Is whistling and the sun is brighter
Than God's own shadow in the cup now!
Forget the hour-bell. Mournful matins
Will sound as well, Patric, at nightfall.

Faintly through mist of broken water
Fionn heard my melody in Norway,
He found the forest track, he brought back
This beak to gild the branch and tell, there,
Why men must welcome in the daylight.

He loved the breeze that warns the black grouse,
The shout of gillies in the morning
When packs are counted and the swans cloud
Loch Erne, but more than all those voices,
My throat rejoicing from the hawthorn.

In little cells behind a cashel,
Patric, no handbell has a glad sound.

But knowledge is found among the branches.
Listen! The song that shakes my feathers
Will thong the leather of your satchels.

Stop, stop and listen for the bough top
Is whistling . . .

IN WICKLOW

The high trees grieve like the sea's water.
The sad sky crouches on Carraig and Slaughter;
And a crude donkey, from the windy quarter
       Calls up the rain.
Sunlight sleeps in the tinker's kettle,
Where twilight-bannered, elfin nettle
And the fool's-parsley's starry clusters battle
       For kingship of the lane.

Clouded waves comb the shadowed shore,
Sifting the sliding shingle for
What, in past time, furnished the sea's floor,
       Seaweed or stone;
And the old gypsy gropes, to find,
Thrown on the foreshore of her mind,
Forgotten things, washed up and left behind—
       Thoughts that were once her own.

POEM

Is to love, this—to nurse a name,
The symbol of a person, of a presence,
As when a novice invokes her saint,
And the sweet title's murmured once every second?

And is it to create, merging the false and true,
A not-impossible world of miracle,
Where intuition strains to know the absolute,
And fantasy seems more certain than things visible?

More than this. Lover and mystic, stirred, spirit-shaken,
Yield to an instant urge, shape the will newly,

35

Take the shock, unresisting, of storm and danger,
Accept the implication of a curve, subdued to the wave's beauty.

THE BRIGHT HILLSIDE

With a gull's beak I cry
    And mount through strong resistance.
My wingspan beats the sky
    Across the high distance,

Circling about your place,
    Wheeling to cover your bed
With the curve of space
    And the airs overhead;

To keep you, to delay
    Spirit in one dear shape;
But spirit will not stay
    When it has planned escape,

And life at last will leave
    This, and all bodies, dead—
Those who remain to grieve:
    The world they habited;

The bushes bared of green,
    The lake waters unfinned,
And the bright hillside clean
    Of any wind.

RUNAWAY

Somebody has got to tell me something real
and that very quickly.
Someone must show me a thing
that will not disappear when I touch it,
or fade into a cloud to walk through

when I have looked at it and
thought about it long enough.

You are not final:
you will be bones.
The feet I see marking the pavements
will walk too long
and not long enough,
and I will see the streets
clean in the morning, (tomorrow morning) after rain;
but the feet that marked the footpaths
will have stepped into the grave,
stepped into the grave,
before I have done with them.

Who is going to tell me where the dark horses of the spirit go?
Have I come into this room now?
Or was I always in this place?
And could you in your speech
have an inference different from mine?
Do you signify, proud other people,
what you appear to be,
or imply quite another meaning in your existence?

Place me on the edge of a cliff
and tell me now where to leap,
for the horses are pulling on the reins—
I have no wish to hold them.

SPRING DOGGEREL

When the shy, slender thrush
Makes arrowy silence as she leaves her tree
And slips to shelter among further boughs;
When long March-morning shadows, spread like veils,
Hinder the grass, and daisies in poor pasture
Lean the same way: when primroses are scarce
And the whole wren shouts in her brave, great song;
Where each white lamb traffics with his own mother,
Spring looks between pencilled trees, as a wayward child
Through her dark, tumbled hair. She wears the dandelion,
Her bodice laced with catkin and with kingcup.

Then cowslips grace the grass, and lazy cattle
Move tortoise necks to lick their spotted flanks;
Then creaking tit and grating chaffinch flit
Within the maybush, and a singing school
Of linnets shakes the blackthorn's rimy lace;
In duck's-foot sycamore the robin sings,
And balanced blackbirds light on yielding twigs.
The water in the shallow ditch is stitched
With thronging minnows, with their shadows; while
From that blurred, blinding loudspeaker sky
Comes pouring like sunlight the lark's noisiest music.

A DREAM

I looked across and beyond the churned-up lake,
Murky under a tattered sky
And someone said, (there was no-one) "There, just there,
    Where the hills dip low,
    Will your cast-off body lie."

"Quiet after your traffickings to and fro,
Hurryings here and there without end,
So very quiet that curlew and grey-lag goose,
Even wild philibín,
    Take it at last for friend."

THE MOUNTAIN TREE

"This is no place for a tree," said the sour black soil,
"Poor lost embryo, soon to perish
Famished, waterlogged, slowly poisoned,
Hypnum, sphagnum, heather and sedge,
These uncouth ones alone I cherish."
But the rock said to the scarlet berry—
"Welcome, friend, here's ample for sharing;
Thrust your roots in my garnered humus,
Search my fissures, my crumbling crystals,
Food is there for your hardy rearing."

"This is no place for a tree," said the mountain sheep,
Horny and speckled, the tireless ranger,
Always questing and never finding,
"Here's one mouthful to stay my hunger."
But the rock said to the green-tipped seedling—
"See how my bastions overhang you!
Reach out your twigs where the swamp lies deepest—

39

Even the supple rapacious horny,
Lacking foot-hold, must vainly long for you."

"This is no place for a tree," said the savage wind,
Storming in from the western ocean,
Battle-drunk as a berserk hero,
Cruel and bitter with gathered sea-salt,
Filling heaven with wild commotion.
But the rock said to the flower-decked sapling,
"Never fear the hurricane's fury,
Brace your roots round my rugged outcrops,
Shelter under my jutting ledges;
Nursling of mine, be strong and wary."

"This is no place for a tree," said the man astray,
Toiling on between cloud and mire,
(Chaos-region, where land and water,
Light and darkness, still wait dividing)—
Knowing only, he must climb higher—
"Such a broad tree, with its lustrous branches,
Never yet grew amongst starveling heather.
This is a beacon set by the great ones,
Angus for beauty and Barr for staunchness—
Under this rock they met together."

ERRIS COAST, 1943

Black Crosses on the skyline, like a squad heedless of levies,
Lean over and hither, rest on each other's shoulders,
While above them the ruined abbey obtrudes its senseless bulk.
    The crosses were raised with pious labour and bedewed with
        tears—
    The church was once a temple full of significant grace—
But set upon by the sea, betrayed by the sand, sense and beauty
        were battered out of them.

Now they stand like vestiges of Earth and Sin against the walls of
        Paradise

Tourmaline, topaz, opal, a hundred cubits of rubies,
Two hundred cubits of refined gold,
Fifty courses of turquoise, and seventy of unburnished silver—
A Heavenly city, built for the sea and sun for their nightly pleasure.

The monks' prayers and the buried men's lives are remembered by
    God,
But men have forgotten them,
Being absorbed in life, in getting and keeping.
The sea is life to them, bringing good gifts and bad,
Kegs of lard, sea-wrack, mines, men without faces,
Who must on no account sail with the fish.
The next bemused generation, absorbed in its own snarls, will have
    forgotten this.
Meanwhile ruins, crosses, the dunes themselves, change and dis-
    solve like the sunset,
And no magic of the elements will rebuild them as the sun and
    ocean rebuild their city daily.

Two things only, ephemeral, valueless,
Drifted in here from Inisglora on the wind,
Will be remembered as long as man stands with his eyes on the
    West—
Two things having some tincture of Eternity—
The sound of Brendan's bell, and the sloughed-off pelt of a wild
    swan.

FABLE

The tale is every time the same
In all essentials—all but name
Of church and parson; comes in each
The moment when he rose to preach
And through the open door came in
The father of lies, the sire of sin,
The Capricorn, the wandering goat,
With tassels dangling at his throat,
With dewy beard and dewy eye
And air more innocent than sly.

The clattering of the cloven hoof
Rang to the rafters of the roof.
They tell, too, how the sight perplexed
The parson as he spoke the text.
Sometimes they say that from his lip
He let some rank expletive slip
That showed him, under fur and frock
A man like all his farming flock.

But others represent him dumb
To see the unhallowed creature come
Up to the pulpit, thence depose
The priest, with soft and sensuous nose
Sniff at the Book, discreetly cough
And carry on where he left off.

—So the tale runs: but all omit
The most noteworthy part of it,
That He, whose omnipresent care
Protects the sparrows of the air,
Should stretch a point and still provide
A guardian angel-hand to guide

His Adversary safely through
Such tempting clumps of churchyard yew.

For this recurring circumstance
The credit must not go to chance.
The moral of which appears to be
That you must keep the platform free
But let your enemy present his case
In the least favourable time and place.

FROM BURTON THE ANATOMIST

A peacock in Leucadia loved a maid;
And through a deep aquarium of shade
    They wandered side by side,
For ilex there and oleander wove
Their cool defences for the sacred grove.
    His fan, the peacock's pride,
Re-formed in shadow for her gentle eyes
The harsh lights of the waters and the skies.
    But when death took the maid
And empty desolation swept those lawns,
The colours of a million dusks and dawns
    Lay low where she was laid.

TWO VOYAGES

I: SUMMER

Leaving the bar slack-watered, I have left
The quiet man in the corner with his pint
    Who did not speak, the hour
    We drank and chatted there.

High walls of granite over-arched with elder
Dividing gardens. Long deserted lanes

Behind the houses. Here
The cats walk warily.

I walk with them to you, who like a cat
Sit curled and purr before an empty grate.
    Two points of light have hailed
    Each other in the night.

II: WINTER

Love's equinoctial gales are past, the path
Along the long lanes leads again through night.
    The trees are bare, the air
    A halo round each lamp.

Gentlest imaginable groundswell heaving
Hardly disturbs the wrack. The wave that broke
    Over us both, has passed,
    And now the calm succeeds.

And now the fire's the focus of the room
By winter made so. Like a gay salute
    There crackles in the hearth
    The holly's fusillade.

LOVE POEM

Flowers upon your lips and hands,
The gentle movement of your breast:
I have remembered these in lands
Where I was but a passing guest.

Strange, to have seen so long before,
Reflected through each flaw and fault,
This inlet on the sunlit shore
Where the sweet water meets the salt.

POEM

High on a ridge of tiles
A cat, erect and lean
Looks down and slyly smiles.
The pointed ears are keen
Listening for a sound
To rise from the back-yard:
He casts upon the ground
A moment's cold regard.

. . . . .

Whatever has occurred
Is on so small a scale
That we can but infer
From the trembling of the tail
And the look of blank surprise
That glares out of the eyes
That underneath black fur
His face is deadly pale.

LESLIE DAIKEN

NOSTALGIE D'AUTOMNE

Island of Shadow
Silk of the Kine
Mouse in the meadow
And crab-apple wine

Sun on the brambles
Rocking a pram
And driving the yellow
Wasps offa the jam

Sugar-pears hangin
Ripe ready to fall
And a lass stringin mushrooms
In warm Donegal

Starlings at sunset
Linnets at noon
And cat-owl and cricket
Cry out with the moon

Island of Shadow
Silk of the Kine
Will Sickle and Hammer
Ever be thine?

Melon and marrow
Stored by the load
Here on a barrow
In Theobald's Road.

LINES TO MY FATHER

You have not left me usurer's black blood
Nor legacy of bawdry or disgrace,
Yet against your own improvidence you could
Have schooled me. You, whose peasant's face,
Grained with the sweat of some grim charioteer,
Disdained to tame fresh horses into fear,
But scared the gazers with high-stepping grace.
Old jobstock-man, you drove with foxy zeal
A merchant's hard, but never haggling, deal:
Here, split a sovereign; there, not a fraction budge
From your inflexible rockbottom fudge
Till those brisk hands, chapped and weather-bit,
Clapped, palm on palm, their stamp of friendly spit
In every City metal-yard or any country pub
And the glass of malt had method . . . Aye, there's the rub
Dead Father! . . . Peace on you, hoarding spendthrift!
Your gambler's blood is in me. Let me drift
Then, down my poet's millrace—to what end?—
Who failed to break a son into a friend.

AN WITH A PINT OF PORTER

JUNE SONG OF A MAN WHO LOOKS TWO WAYS

As the coin of her ear-ring
Her ear-lobe adorns,
So droop the wild fucshia
At the nape of the Mournes.

Her heart flowers secret,
Deep, delicately,
So yields the snap-dragon
To the urge of the bee.

As the tiller can tell in
The may's lavish yield
The fruit of his orchard
And pasture and field,

I know that high harvests
Must banner the birth
Of our love's panorama
With beauty and worth.

Then, fuse on the coin of
My heart's imagery,
June, fuchsia and ear-lobe,
Snapdragon and bee.

WHERE THE DROPWORT SPRINGS UP LITHE AND TALL

Where the dropwort springs up lithe and tall,
And a thunder mounts from the waterfall;
Where the salmon pass from the salted seas,
And the hook-billed birds come down the breeze,
    If she look in the dark and thund'rous pool,
    She will see his body in spindrift cool.

Where the pigeons beat with heavy wings,
And the weasel wars with the furry things;
Where the lizard lies in the grasses still,
And the spider spins gold cloth on the hill;
    If she stumble on through the thick growths there,
    She will feel his heartbeats in sun and air.

GLENARM

Past ploughed and fallow, at the top
Of the glen where stunted hazels grow,
With pensive show
Of white moss-banded arms that drop,
Wind-struck, into the daisy crop;
There, on a thought, the first doe would rise
With daisy meads in her two eyes.

Past forest bridge and up the slope
Where slim and straight the hazels grow,
But closer now,
Ringstraked with light and all a-drop
With dazzling mist until you stop;
There, at a sound, the last stag would rise
With hazel woods in his two eyes.

THE HERON

At night, when the black water-hen
    Roosts by the first star,
The heron stands, a lonely king,
    Where his possessions are:
The level flag-torn mere,
    The oozy yellow lands,
The shells that thicken on the rocks
    And blacken on the sands.
His shadow's length away from him—
    Shadowed in the moon rays—
Is she whom the subtle unknown love
    Brought to his lonely ways.
Sometimes, askance, he sees the bright
    Moon-silver float
Slow cones and arrows from her body;
    But long ago the note
Of triumph went from him and still
    When life exults and sings,
A broken water-sound pursues
    His trailing feet and wings.

.   .   .   .   .   .

I knew the heron in his nest,
    His voice not yet a cry,
When he lay on the flat spare twigs
    And watched the sun in the sky.

SEEING

Logic is my eye:
    which seams the hills;
    which runs between the halves of a seed and parts the two-
        lobed earth;
    which splits the clover-leaf and flakes the day-beam;

which preserves the creases on the shell of liquid fire,
and has crystal children of the sky.

Symmetry is my glass:
    by which I walk earth's hidden wing;
    by which I have an inkling of violet-starry crown and preg-
        nant numbers spilling from the poppy womb;
    by which I take spirit on a cross of ivory, as spindrift is
        taken on twigs;
    by which I walk in Eden through a growth of coloured light,
        disengaging the fruits of flame,
and am at the end of soul's endless journey.

THE GRAVE

The country folk who pass have said to me,
That thirteen seasons must bury the beloved,
Before the tomb's secure, the fugitive
Hid well away, although the pit's filled in,
The squat, dwarf railings rusted round the grave.

Now, well may all that they have said be true,
Well even her spirit find the Christian Heaven,
Well even her loosened members reassemble
At Michael's trump, wearing her look and smile,
And well may all that they have said be lies—
But there's no aeon's clingy clay with power
To protect the casket given it in charge
From tunnelling otter, or grave rat and worm
That minister to death in closest chambers,
Answering at last, though hindered long from office,
The thud of burial clay;
                    and there's no earth,
No sexton season's care, to hide the box,
Even now, from scratching ravens of the mind.

EBB

The past is fresh, dust is fresh—
    oh, the colour and light that is in a heap of sand—
    on the sand dunes crystal glaciers slide,
    battalions of tiny stars fret softly together.

Flung on the sand dunes, in the brilliant light,
    I grip fistfuls of shiney particles
    and crush them again with force through my fingers,
    and ponder the broken dazzle of minutes.

Oh, more marvellous still, the fire immured
    in pores of agaric-grown ruin,
    purple and grey-green and orange.

Where fall is delicate I pass
    and put my hands by the foot of sombre-glowing stones,
    gay trunks, and spotty leaves,
    to gather the fine shower
    and dream of the invisible dropping away of ages.

For the sand falls
    with a broken dazzle—
    a showery sparkle of diamond,
but the dust sinks
    like loosened pearl
    in a tide softly.

THE FOSSIL

Dream of the walls of a cave,
     our souls a slake of lime,
     at every pore of the rock
     streamily oozing.
Hush! there must be silence round,
     the tide of eternity flow
          in from the ocean,
     only light bringing
          in at the cave mouth.

Very still! let the ocean swell,
     and dampness rise through the rock.
The mouth of the cave shall be stopped
     with a full and soft lit swell
                    from fields
     of the dark blue blossom of sea—
     night shall be ever present and day
               be ever the same.

But the slake of lime, like sweat, shall break from roof and wall,
     till the roof is dropped all over with drops of milky ooze,
     that inly dregs and sheds pure water off,
     and ever marbling ever flows,
     while downward from the roof
     and upward from the ground
     a frail column grows—

and in the rifts the milky surge is poured,
     and at the edge a dewy drip begun,
     that ever marbling ever drips,
     while downward from the ledge
     and upward from the ground
     a thin warp is spun.

Then, like a woof, the sides of the cave shall stream
     with flaky scum from the rock,

and a glaze come over the inkiness
  with glassy mallow hues,
and the silver dreg and the mauve,
  till the crevices here and there
  are crossed with purple spar.

Dream of the walls of a cave,
  our souls a slake of lime,
  at every pore of the rock
  streamily oozing.

Till we come by in other sort
  and break it like a stone,
and joy to see the crystal web
  within its cave-like shell.

WRITING ON THE WALL

Throw something to the gulls, any old scrap
As you go down the quays when the day awakes!
Throw something to the gulls, they are so quiet, so keen,
In those white minutes when the dawn breaks
With a soft feathery explosion.

Anything, a bit of unblessed bread, throw it
To the gulls; throw something to the gulls.
Though they seem dropped bright feathers of dawn, a poet
knows better. They are no eddying snowflakes,
But bellies, appetites.

Throw something then, a pennyweight of bread!
Before one preying beak can gather it between
Wind and water, thousands are round your head,
A tumult, a squawking crown, wind-blown;
You are caught in a storm.

Cast your bread upon those waters. It will return
In a foam of birds that scrawls upon the air
A luminous word that will leave you insecure—
Wondering how belly-hunger with this quill of spray and storm
Could forge such a dazzling signature.

LONG JOHN

'On royal crowns and purples, I
Might stake the long purse of my soul,
But, say, if bad luck turned the wheel,'
        Said that tramper John Mulroy,
'The devil might get me in the heel.

So on this sunny hill I'll loll,
My long knees wandering up the sky,
And think while clouds drift through my knees
That no crown's worth a moment's ease.'

'Yet, had I that red-haired woman
Who queened in Cruachan long ago
And loved all gambling gallant men,'
                    Sighed that rambler, John,
'I'd have the great times in Mayo.
But, say, would I be better then?
For would my work be ever done
In keeping off the other men?
And think! O white cloud on my knee!
Of that responsibility.'

'Now that the young year's spun her coin
Into the sun and speckled bees
Hive the dripping summer here,'
                    Yawned that rascal John,
'The noise of farming in the leas
Is pleasing to a drowsy ear,
And as I stretch out I must own
That hives and farmers shut my eyes
As well as mother's lullabies.'

LADY DAY

In the low house, whose thick lights
Laboured each day to take true casts of her
Brown face with its thin high bones, she washed before the fire
Like a queen inside a penny:
And there as she did her hair in an old green glass
The room bloomed and was stirred so delicately
That the dead in their photographs seemed coming alive
In their stiff Sunday finery
And flushed old masks of paper and acid where time
Decayed by sad shades into Purgatory.

YACHTS ON THE HARD

And there, as she stepped from one dress into another
In the tremors and rays of
A reverie as quietly electric as the Great Emperor Moth's,
One feared that the men for miles
Would arrive with beating hands at the little window
Out of the stirring countryside;
But nothing happened; demurely she steps out with
A maid's mouth and a maid's eyes
Past hens asleep in their wings and a sow in a fat grunt
And cycles off into the skies.

And the slow afternoon big and blue
Lifted in hazy hackles from her shoulders;
Moving, she trailed the sky too
Over crops and cattle;
And out of the ripening fields which she spread
Like a peacock's tail, so very small in
That huge plumage of smoky country, she
Advances to the Pattern;
Her black hair combed to the scalp
Brilliant as oil on water.

She picked a calm way through
Mourners and merrymakers where I waited
With the warm airs piled like sweet hay on the new
Mown graves of the parish dead,
And there as promised I sought her among the neighbours—
To find in group after group her twin instead,
O sequence of sisters! O cool stone shedding comets!
Wherever my dazzled eye stayed
Some girl in her very image stared at me and smiled
With the same red mouth, brown eyes, and small black head.

O believe me I counted one, three others and three more,
Seven, and each face hers, as I mooned around
Like a fool from soft stare to soft stare
Confounded and distressed
And nervous, yes, and afraid, as if from the skies that holyday
One mocked me with a sinister and subtle jest
And made this bright face common as seven scraps of mirror

That her own face should rest
In its large drift from Nazareth alone
Over the harvest and be blest.

Would you blame me, badgered as I was, for taking a glass
With the other men until sun-down
Called them to lonely farmsteads with the tongue-tied speech of
    grass?
And then among their farewells,
Away there, ah my eyes opened, one sauntered before me
With the afterglow slung like a skirt from her calm hips!
But though I followed her and though she came
Under the elms with me and into my arms,
Alas, I am not certain which of the seven has left me
Those images that sweat upon the lenses of my palms.

And may the mother who nurses my music strangle me
For a lout if I could ask her
If she were the girl who promised so shyly
To meet me that afternoon,
So innocently that no country mother would dare
Pass with a buttoned mouth and looks black as soutanes:
No, I will not believe it, no!
But could I ask for that assurance
When the night with all stops stirring died away
Into itself like stilled melodeons?

And torn with doubt and exultance I will mention
No more of her save to declare
That Adam with his teeth in the pips would envy
The soft shock of her mouth:
Yet, even as she left me, I was wondering sadly
If another who had promised me more innocent hours
Might be rubbing out the black miles home on her bicycle
That moment with pain on her brows.
O desolate cypher of starlight!
No planet in your sunken house.

OUT OF SOUNDINGS

When noon is warm, old Pensioners
Come one by one to the sea-wall,
Copper or bleak bleached men in bowler hats
Rolling a spit, deep-water sailors;
Old eyes, old wits,
Old illnesses, they take them for a stroll:
Good-morrow! Aye, quite hearty—on the whole.

And here they are, the deep-water men,
Palming calm words with their pipes like clay-footed farmers;
They, whose words should be harsh birds squawking from the
    living chart
Under their skins where things still happen,
Decline the effort,
And something unique and barbarous
In their hollow middles perishes.

If their flesh were accurate they would sweat
Oceans in bold blue bruises, their heads
Would glitter like mercury and glass, and I
Could take the sun as in a sextant
From each blazing eye,
And guess the whole wild atlas with its blues and reds
Ere they leave it, useless in the linen, on their last bedsteads.

I'd be their climate, or soft wax to them, or blotting paper;
But, now, as death upholsters their old bodies,
They perish into dolls;
And a world, brutal as wounds, that scored each nerve-centre
Sudden as the bright beaks of gulls,
Contracts, and day-by-day dies
Almost before my eyes.

I search down their innocent indolent stares,
And they say goodmorning, or yes the wind will rise;
I catch at their minds and they hang limp

In my fingers as empty coat-collars,
Or disgorge with a dry hard rattle simple
And wooden replies
Like toy ships for schoolboys.

And never, though I cherished them, have I sensed on some bared
    nerve,
Dim as in an old green bottle, miraculously
A skyline surge with a great ship—
And had six old men around me in a surf
Of raving radiance, striking hip
And thigh for words to make me see
A god by proxy.

O for all their wings and winds, big ships sink into calluses,
Smaller than butterflies, as a sailor's hands grow hard;
Just as early love sinks, whose breasts were white pigeons
With small red bills,
Into woman after woman in the dockside dens
Till it leers at last, a poxed nightbird
With a drunken feather-boa, from a dirty word.

If they grope, tattooed with their night-sweats, from terrible beds
Of geography every morning into bodies
Wrung with their manias like a too-much worn underwear,
Here they are quiet men with hats on their heads,
So peaceful that light, like a gull, can settle on each gesture—
Almost nonentities:
This is how time dies.

And knowing that their hands should revolt and break into clouds
Of sails, that their backs should arch in thunder,
And their tongues, O barbarous chanteymen, find for their harsh
    days
Words that would break their mouths
Sideways like paralysis, yet all that I say is
Good-morning as I pass, and they answer me fair,
Good-morning, goodmorning, goodmorning—sir.

ELEGY FOR A COUNTRYMAN

He made no history, even
At home in one quiet townland
Where the houses, so still in thatch and lime, are lost
In the hazy stir
And murmur of all green Ireland.

He was never a speaker at meetings,
Nor, masked among Moonlighters,
Never broke walls and scattered a landlord's herd;
Nor, later, if he heeded them,
Was he one with the Gunfighters.

Why then should I think and think of you
And talk of you to strangers
When the priest of the parish forgot your name before
High Mass was over and your body laid
Down obscurely with your nameless fathers?

Only that in your quiet image, brother,
So many gentle wise-eyed men awake
Over lonely fields and forlorn farmhouses
And stare at me till I speak and speak
Lest my heart break.

THE STOLEN FIFER

I was brought up in a rampart
On the top of a slieve where the heart
Had its wine-fill of Beauty once.
I was brought up in a trance.

By this-one and that-one, a-near, and a-far
I was brought up by the moon and the star
And the sun and the wave of the sea and the one
Sky of the good and the pure and the free.

I was brought up in a tower.
I was brought up with the poor and the done
Old man and the wind of the shee
Did not find it hard on their power
To weave the web of dream over me.

Now I am locked in the doon
And the people of wing and of wind and of wine
Sing to me at the rise of the moon
And sing to me till the last star shine.

And I am a boy forever from growing
And I am a man forever from sowing
And no man knows what I be knowing
When wind is on the pine and blowing.

I was brought up on top of a slieve
And can not live on the earth, for the town
Of the earth, which I do not believe
In, pulls me down, pulls me down.

DERANGED

Liefer would I turn and love
The ox in the by-path, the sloe on the bush
Than take to the blithe creature would crush
  All in her hands!

It is fitting not for a young man
To turning of face backward like this
Carrying a cut from the knife of her kiss,
  The smart of her lips!

O comely indeed the arrangement of her hair!
Beyond that the ease of her shoulder,
Her two blue eyes: nothing bolder!
  Her two blue eyes!

O moonlight that wasted me, O harsh little stars:
Sharp cutting reproaches from what tongue could not say!
She left me alone one scald of a day,
  The deceit of the one!

Liefer would I turn and love
The ox in the by-path, the barn-yard dove!

THE POET

I am the chaunt-rann of a Singer
Who has sung to heart at night
How the rust-loch's hazel waters
    Mirror the stars all right:
    Christ on a tree for you and me
    And the moon-dark worlds between!

I am the chaunt-rann of a Singer
Who has sung to heart by day
How the grey rain on the wet street
    Washes our lives away:
    Christ on a tree for you and me
    And the sun-bright worlds between!

I am the chaunt-rann of a Singer
Who does not cease chaunt with loam
As the crouched lime of the good earth
    Eats us away on home:
    Christ on a tree for you and me
    And none of the worlds between!

THE BOY AND THE GEESE

The swans rise up with their wings in day
And they fly to the sky like the clouds away;

Yet with all their beauty and grace and might
I would rather have geese for their less-smooth flight.

I would rather have geese for they're ugly like me
And because they are ugly, as ugly can be
I would rather have geese for their mystery.

THE SHAWLS

They'll walk no longer to Mass on Sunday,
In groups or single, sleek-tressed or grey,
The black shawl gathered round head and shoulder.
The shawls are few upon Easter Day.

The islands bring them in boat and curragh,
Rowing early across the bay;
The bog still clings to the ancient custom,
But the shawls are fewer each Easter Day.

Had a young girl grace, had she pride of carriage,
Had her glance a meaning grave or gay,
The shawl revealed it, for nought could hide it
When they queened it simply this April day.

Lovely the face that hid its secret,
Lifted in laughter or stooped to pray,
The brow laid bare and the cheek half-curtained,
Till shawls were banished on Easter Day.

I met a woman of sixty summers,
Her road before her a lengthy way,
I turned to stare like a young man dumbstruck,
For the shawl grows rarer from day to day.

That snow-white hair, which the brown shawl slipped from,
Those eyes still clear as a sky in May,
That noble forehead—were cause to sorrow
That shawls should vanish this Holy Day.

Is beauty lost that they hope to purchase
Its shreds and semblance? There were times, I'll say,
When they stepped it lightly with eyes more flashing,
And hearts more carefree, where joy held sway.

The boats are launching. The Mass is over.
The road is crowded, the sky is grey.
I lingered, thinking of heads held higher
When shawls were many—on Easter Day.

FRENCH PEASANTS

These going home at dusk
Along the lane,
After the day's warm work,
Do not complain.

Were you to say to them,
"What does it mean?
What is it all about,
This troubled dream?"

They would not understand,
They'd go their way,
Or, if they spoke at all,
They'd surely say,

"Dawn is the time to rise,
Days are to earn
Bread and the mid-day rest,
Dusk to return;

"To be content, to pray.
To hear songs sung,
Or to make wayside love,
If one is young.

"All from the good God comes,
All then is good;
Sorrow is known to Him,
And understood."

One who had questioned all,
And was not wise,
Might be ashamed to meet
Their quiet eyes.

All is so clear to them,
All is so plain,
These who go home at dusk,
Along the lane.

FOREBEARS

Peasants my forebears were,
Say what you will;
The peasant blood was there,
And lingers still.

The peasant's thrift and care,
His prudent toil,
His love of simple things,
And of the soil.

Their days were calmly spent,
Their nights were long;
The joy they felt they'd hum
In some old song.

These are the men whose blood
Runs in my veins,
Well used to summer heat
And autumn rains.

Country physician, clerk,
Or clergyman,
It was the land they loved,
The land loved them.

Horses and dogs they held
As good as men,
Their pockets filled with crumbs
For some stray hen.

Books that were to their taste
They too would read;
Speech was a luxury,
Silence a need.

And even I who seem
To break that line,
Have moments when I wish
A small field mine,

Will stop on sunny days
And pleasure feel
To see some fowl at work
On a dunghill.

Or in a doorway stand,
The dim cow-shed
Pleasing me with its stalls
Where beasts are fed:

Watch them slow-munching now
Their share of hay,
Breathe the warm air they've breathed
Nor move away;

Can while a morning through
With this allure,
Or from a hill can watch
Them spread manure

Across a field from those
Small heaps near by,
Where the farm-cart had stopped
To let them lie.

These are the moments when
My heart makes free
To praise the very men
Who'd disown me,

To praise the very men
To whom a rhyme
That took a morning's work
Were waste of time.

SONG

Singer within the little streets,
Sing her a song about a fool who came,
Looked in her eyes, and in that moment knew
Nothing would be the same

Ever again, a fool who hardly knew
When the stars shone, or when the slanting rain,
Beat on his face, or anything at all,
Or any pain

Save the one pain—to-morrow might not come,
Or any fear—save that he should be blind,
Or any thought—save that her words were sweet,
Her eyes were kind.

WISER THAN THE CHILDREN OF LIGHT

Shelley, madman, made his rhymes,
And let the world spit on his name,
Knowing he who honour seeks
Careless grows of present fame.

Never on that damask cheek
Did fortune print a passing kiss;
He who lives for that world learns
His duty is to die to this.

So Blake affirmed if earthly glory
Had passed him by he should be glad,
Since all such glory means the less
In spiritual worlds is had.

Their names are gold in all mouths now,
They reap a crop neglect did sow;
But men prefer to take the cash
And let such fragile credit go.

THE BIRD

I.

A bird flew tangent-wise to the open window.
His face was a black face of black, unknowing death;
His eyes threw the grim glint of sharpened stones,
That children pile by unfrequented roads.

And that night, dreaming into a rapture of cardboard life,
I started at the lean face of the bird:
A crow I think it was; but it was also death:
And sure enough there was the crisp telegram next morning.

I placed my mirror to the flat, unfiltered light,
But the razor cut me, in spite of the guarantee;
And I knew it was not the razor, but the ebony beak,
That slashed the base of my left nostril.

II.

I loved the man who lay in the cheap coffin.
It was he first showed me the damp, stereoscopic fields
Of County Down; and now he was away to farm
The curving acres of his jealous God.

I loved the ploughing of his sun-caught brow,
And the hay-lines, and chicken-feathers in his hair,
That was hay itself; the strongly cobbled boots,
And the swaying, coloured idiom of his mind.

And now he was lying with the Holy Bible under his chin,
Sorry only to have died before harvest and peat-cutting:
Lying dead in the room of rafters, and the gray, stopped clock—
Because of the hatred of the bird I did not kill.

III.

Sometimes now, years after, I am nakedly afraid in mid-winter,
And ashamed to be afraid of an incessant beak,
That raps a symphony of death on the window-panes,
Of the window I dare not throw wide open.

But one evening, just before I go to bed to die,
There will be the black face of black, unknowing death,
Flying past my open window; there will be the black bird
With poison in his beak, and hatred in his wings . . .

THE FAR COUNTRY

There is a far country where there is a hall for dreams
And the taut hopes of men who have sweated in the sun;
You will find a lake for cooling and for healing
The jibes and bruises of the dour machines.

It is no country for School Captains, healthy thinkers,
Men with salt-and-pepper minds, ribbons on their hearts:
Only for the hungry and halt and humbled
Do these white switchback lanes, those careless meadows open . . .

Over there no one shall seek escape and no one
Shall break in agony or bend under the unjustified load,
Over there all may swim in the lake of cooling,
And sins peel off as slimy film from skeleton.

There in the far country there is a niche for dreams,
But not for going and getting, or praying and petting,
But you will find no salt in the lake that is not lacking,
And life will peel away, will fall and wither and peel away.

WRITTEN ON THE SENSE OF ISOLATION IN CONTEMPORARY IRELAND

The Irish faults are not so very new,
We're still that vainly violent, lawless crew
Whose generous verve leaves all to chance
But seldom halts the irregular advance.
Think now of all the unfettered great
In heart and mind, who gave no inch to fate.
There savage, tender Swift whose burning mind
Only lewd chaos finally could bind.
There Burke the orator, with urbane Sheridan
Jostles to head the bright, uncensored van.
And Congreve, Goldsmith and the verseman Moore
Shall make the Anglo-Irishry endure.
Yeats' shadow falls across the Liffey still
Pressing its callous spell on lyrist will.
Yet all of these the world for subject took
And wed the fearless thesis to their book.
To-day the yes-men glimmer in pretence,
Secure in their own dribbling competence:
While those who speak with honest passion
Are freezed-out devotees of spendthrift fashion.
These figures crowd around: their angry ghosts
Smash down the glasses at the dunces' toasts.

So now in days of fevered fret and stress
Let Europe measure out our Irishness!

MICHAEL WALKED IN THE WOOD

Michael walked in the green wood
With his friends in buzzing summer
And they talked economics
And art in the clover.

To animal noises of secretive woodland
Michael was listening between the grim strictures.
In the grey-blanket sky, pebbled with blue
One voice sang in sad pictures—

'Like a leaf in the city wind
Brief man is blown
From pavement to pavement
In drab discontent.

'Like a petal he falls
On the river's fake silver,
Soundless he perishes
Without a farewell.

'Like a tree in a storm
His roots are struck out
And the grass ever-cunning
Firms down the torn earth.

'Like a leaf in city September
He eddies and eddies.
Brief man is blown
From pavement to pavement . . .'

Michael talked in the green wood
With his friends in their summer
And they walked as they talked
Among ferns and bracken and clover.

THE GLORIOUS TWELFTH

(July 12, 1943)

You will remember that the Twelfth was always dry,
That rain followed the day after, some said as Judgment,
While others argued that drums of Ulster stirring
Pulled out the corded wetness from our local skies.
Four years ago we heard them last, heard the thunder
Smouldering through the ribboned streets towards the battle
In the fields of Finaghy. There was fire then,
Fire in our throats, fire beaten out from our cities,
Cold, distant, strongly arid in the normal weather:
Four years ago since last we heard the drums' thunder,
Since the Orange banners looped in gay procession
And bands of flute and fife, of brass and silver
Played hell to the Pope and immortality to William—
To William, Prince of Orange, defender and avenger,
To William, the stiff Dutch Protestant who saved us
From villainous James, the tyrant Stuart King.

Remember 1690, remember the ancient wrongs of Rome,
Remember Derry, Aughrim, Enniskillen and the Boyne,
The glorious Boyne in Ireland, where the Pope was overcome,
Remember the Maiden City and the breaking of her boom.

These were my people marching on the streets,
Released from inhibition and resolved to keep the faith.
Four years have passed since Ulster opened up her heart,
And toasted her deliverance from the Seven Hills,
Four years since fire has run swift rivers into Europe
From Dunkirk to Briansk, from Naples to Novgorod,
From Caucasus to Clyde, from Warsaw to Belfast.
And now, in Derry and Downpatrick no Ulstermen are marching
To the rustle of their banners and the flogging of their drums.
Our red-brick cities have their blackened skeletons,
Our people carry the public and the personal wound.

Forgotten 1690, forgotten the ancient wrongs of Rome,
Forgotten Derry, Aughrim, Enniskillen and the Boyne,
The glorious Boyne in Ireland where the Pope was overcome,
Forgotten the Maiden City and the breaking of her boom.

You will remember that the Twelfth was always dry,
While now in Italy the bloods of Continents are joined,
While now the Russian plains are stacked with corpses,
Rotting in the Red sun, feeding plagues to common rats. . . .
But after carnage there will be music; after death will be hope,
After the horror of the day will come the evening dream,
After hatred's harvest joy will march, shrouded, to Finaghy.

CHEZ MADAME

Eternity encountered on the stair
chains and enchants me—standing there, I see
the tide of green, that, crowned with foaming blossom,
leaps all around the house, come seeping through
each crack and crevice in the walls until,
drowned in a scented silence, world is one,
undying, indivisible, complete.

O moment of strange certainty, if I
could only compass you and hold you fast,
I'd cling to you as close as any lover;
but time compels and I must leave you, climb
to my uneasy room set high above
the sombre city that will never cease
its lost unhappy crying in the night.

JOURNEY

Grey in the sky and blue against the trees,
    the long smoke lingers, then is blown
back to the bleak arrested goodbye gesture
on the departure platform. Yellow flowers
pinstripe the green embankment as it rolls
    relentless miles between us.

And now, across the border where the present
    flows to the frozen past, I bring
those free-of-duty moments we have known
and keep them safe in mind, while other thoughts
elude me and go drifting out of sight
    like the receding fields.

81

AFTER THE SHOW

To-night, the gaudy auditorium
echoed applause as gay comedians told
their bawdy jokes; then, clicking castanets
in a fantastic tango, came the quick
tap-dancer stepping with staccato feet.

But, walking homewards through September mist,
I can remember most the still delight
in which the singer held the hall, and how
she gave again to every exile there
the land he lost, the girl he left behind.

And I am lonely suddenly, and sad,
watching the shadow shapes of passers-by
drift softly into darkness like my wishes,
knowing that autumn's in the air and feeling
cheated of all the summer should have brought.

POEM

This room is very old and very wise—
we can do nothing to surprise her now
for, being well acquainted with the dead,
she knows the living intimately, takes
their every mood for granted and accepts
each moment's joy or sorrow as it comes.

See how, chameleon-like, she imitates
the sombre colour of our present thoughts,
so alien and so difficult to grasp,
and how she makes the sunlight on her walls
appear remote and cold, as though she were
the dwelling-place of fear since time began.

RAIN

The theme of morning was the sound of rain,
a sighing monotone involving all
our thoughts in sadness till it seemed as though
the clouds would never pass—yet afternoon
brought welcome respite and we ventured out
to comb the winter air with swinging fingers
and tread the dead year's wreckage underfoot.

I cannot say what road we took or where
the miracle occurred—I only know
that suddenly, as we were walking there,
time, like a door, flew open to disclose
the sunlit continents of love, a world
whose beauty and whose bounty were for us
to rifle, spend or squander, if we chose.

But I had little choice. Alone that night,
I heard the voices of the rain resume
their plaintive lamentation on a note
of even deeper pain—I hear them still
grieving with me that, from our promised land
of riches, I should tear myself away
clutching a beggar's penny in my hand.

MEETING

So you came
with a hyacinth, a poem and a thousand kisses,
and it was spring.

Outside, the city
drew her evening-cloak of velvet closer
about her shoulders

and turned away
into the shadows, while I in your arms' haven
lay safe at last,

knowing that this
was holy ground, that no pursuing ghost
could claim us now.

SONNET

Since I keep only what I give away
Yet give away that which I would not keep,
How else should I, a miserable bankrupt, pay
That old beggar, save with a purse of sleep,
Or with some nodding conversation boil
A tardy pot to stay his hungry maw
Under a tree some evening, or uncoil
Tedious recitals of the law;
How, if he grow importunate at last,
Knock in my door and shake my empty bins
Other than with vague stories of the past
Abate his just and angry claims?
                       O Sins,
Lie down and sleep a little while, lie down;
The hour is late, and far that shining town.

SONNET

Now keep that long revolver at your side
The chambers full, dry-clean, the action cocked;
Sandbag the windows, see the doors are locked,
Set all the fuses, time them and decide
The minute and the hour. Be patient; pride
Demands a shattered wall, a ruined keep,
A trinket for posterity, a cheap
Excursion to the mudheap where you died.

Cut out the loopholes, test their fields of fire,
Survey the ground, select your last retreat:
Somewhere between the earthwork and the wire
There is a foxhole where the meadowsweet
Will fold your anguish in a flowery net
And when you sleep be your sad coverlet.

PALM HOUSE, BOTANIC GARDENS

Monstrous, uncouth, their vast leaves amply spread
Beneath the ribbéd glass, the great trees drowse
While from the soil that holds Glasnevin's dead
They draw the sap that feeds their foreign boughs.

About their scaly boles we celebrate
The solemn northside Sunday afternoon:
Above, in sultry air, their fronds await,
Patient, athirst in vain, the lost monsoon.

This is their refuge; from the gales' assault,
The ravages of locust, drought, disease,
Freedom forever in this glazéd vault,
This tomb, this dungeon: O castrated trees!

JOHN HEWITT

THE GLENS

Groined by deep glens and walled along the west
by the bare hilltops and the tufted moors,
this rim of arable that ends in foam
has but to drop a leaf or snap a branch
and my hand twitches with the leaping verse
as hazel twig will wrench the straining wrists
for untapped jet that thrusts beneath the sod.

Not these my people, of a vainer faith
and a more violent lineage. My dead
lie in the steepled hillock of Kilmore
in a fat country rich with bloom and fruit.
My days, the busy days I owe the world,
are bound to paved unerring road and rooms
heavy with talk of politics and art.
I cannot spare more than a common phrase
of crops and weather when I pace these lanes
and pause at hedge gap spying on their skill
so many fences stretch between our minds.

I fear their creed as we have always feared
the lifted hand between the mind and truth.
I know their savage history of wrong
and would at moments lend an eager voice,
if voice avail, to set that tally straight.

And yet no other corner in this land
offers in shape and colour all I need
for sight to torch the mind with living light.

THE LITTLE LOUGH

There in a bare place, in among the rocks,
grey rounded boulders shouldered from the ground,
where no field's big enough to yield three stacks
and corn grows on a fistful of black land,
is a small narrow lake, narrow and brown,
with whistling rushes elbowed here and there
and in the middle is a grassy stone
that heron or some other wanderer
will rest on darkly. Sometimes there will rise
a squawking mallard with a startling spray,
heading far inland, that the swift eyes lose
in the low mist that closes round the day.

Tho' many things I love should disappear
in the black night ahead of us, I know
I shall remember, silent, crouching there,
your pale face gazing where the rushes grow
seeking between the tall stems for the last
black chick the grebe is cruising round to find,
my pointing finger showing it not lost
but sheltered only from the ruffling wind.

FROST

With frost again the thought is clear and wise
that rain made dismal with a mist's despair;
the raw bleak earth beneath cloud-narrowed skies
finds new horizons in the naked air.
Light leaps along the lashes of the eyes;
a tree is truer for its being bare.

So must the world seem keen and very bright
to one whose gaze is on the end of things,

FARM—COUNTY LIMERICK

who knows, past summer lush, brimmed autumn's height,
no promise in the inevitable springs,
all stripped of shadow down to bone of light,
the false songs gone and gone the restless wings.

POEM IN MAY

May afternoon with birds in every bush
and the hot walls forgotten, I surrender
my tired mind, callous with slack rhetoric
and close to terror at the sick world's plight,
to this clean kingdom vehement with life
that does not need my wrist to crank its gears
but marks its rich and independent hours
with ebb and flow of perfume and of colour,
its little threads of being, chords of motion,
as restlessly complex as evening swarm
of summer midges by a drifting stream.

I lay my senses bare, uncritical,
to be possessed, enjoyed, and laid aside,
and taken up enhanced another time,
not only by my avaricious mind,
but by the swift sensations that themselves
have schooled a surer temper of response.

The life about me, from the humming ground
its gay green gemmed with yellow pimpernel,
with bracken still involved, its rusted whorls
as fat as caterpillars, to the trees
heavy with blossom, thick with singing leaves,
and the high sky a quivering dome of light,
so overcrowds the senses that I sink
into a friendly pantheistic dream
that offers healing and eternity
secure from pain, did not the diligent
and plodding mind, not yet relaxed, insist
on small half-hearted efforts to define

the interwoven strands, the elements
that fused, create a unity beyond
the simple aggregation of their sum:
the chaffinch with his sturdy string of notes
that quavers at the end beyond his reach;
the limestone-loving neat forget-me-not
close to my toe; the moss that cracks the rock
the frosts have menaced, on whose ragged edge
I hoist my limbs; the sycamore above
that holds a birdsong still anonymous
to my poor essay, counterpointed by
the chiff-chaff's seesaw pulsing monotone,
and all the sounds and colours that surround
the hard stone of my heart like endless rings
a pebble wakens in a sleepy pond.

FIRST CORNCRAKE

We heard the corncrake's call from close at hand,
and took the lane that led us near the noise;
a hedged half-acre, flanked by sycamore,
was his small wedge of world. We crouched and peered
through the close thorn. The moving cry again
swivelled our gaze. Time whispered in the leaves.
A tall ditch-grassblade rocked as a languid bee
brushed the dry sliver with a rasping wing.

In silence still we watched; a careless heel
smashing a twig husk, grating on the grit,
and winning for itself a warning glance.
Then, when strung patience seemed about to yawn
as if the world demanded leave to move
on its slung reeling pitch about the sun,
I saw a head, a narrow pointed head
stirring among the brown weed-mottled grass
as the monotonous and edgey voice
kept up its hard complaint. I held the spot
in a fixed gaze. The brown head disappeared,

was seen in seconds in another clump,
and for a blessed moment, full in sight
the brown bird, brighter than the book foresaw,
stood calling in a little pool of grass.
I moved a finger and you shared the joy
that chance till then had never offered us.

It would have been a little grief to know
this punctual cry each year, and yet grow old
without one glimpse of him who made the cry.
The heart still hankers for the rounded shape.

LEAF

O Fall of the leaf, I am tired,
with the sunset let me be still.
The tips of the stubble are fired
by the slanted blade of the sun
sheathing his flame in the hill.
Let me smoulder so and be done.

The withered leaf tumbles and turns
over lazy islands of air,
more lovely now as it burns
than when it was green overhead.
Let me draw from autumnal despair
the strength to be tired without dread.

The pigeons, a dozen and two,
take a half-mile circle of light:
they are washed in the green and the blue
and the delicate gold of the sky.
Let me narrow in on my night
with that effortless certainty.

LYRIC

Let but a thrush begin
or colour catch my eye,
maybe a spring-woke whin
under a reeling sky,

and all at once I lose
mortality's despair,
having so much to choose
out of the teeming air.

THE SWATHE UNCUT

As the brown mowers strode across the field
shapes fled before them thrusting back the grain,
till in a shrinking angle unrevealed
the frightened hare crouched back, the last at bay,
for even the corncrake, blind in his dismay,
had found the narrow safety of the drain.

And so of old the country folk declared
the last swathe holds a wayward fugitive,
uncaught, moth-gentle, tremulously scared,
that must be, by the nature of all grain,
the spirit of the corn that should be slain
if the saved seed will have the strength to live.

Then by their ancient ritual they sought
to kill the queen, the goddess, and ensure
that her spent husk and shell be safely brought
to some known corner of beneficence,
lest her desired and lively influence
be left to mock the next plough's signature.

So I have figured in my crazy wit
is this flat island sundered to the west
the last swathe left uncut, the blessed wheat
wherein still free the gentle creatures go
instinctively erratic, rash or slow,
unregimented, never yet possessed.

ONCE ALIEN HERE

Once alien here my fathers built their house,
claimed, drained, and gave the land the shapes of use,
and for their urgent labour grudged no more
than shuffled pennies from the niggard store
of well rubbed words that had left their overtones
in the ripe England of the mounded downs.

The native Irish limping to the hills
bore with them the enchantments and the spells
that in the clans' free days hung gay and rich
on every twig of every thorny hedge,
and gave the rain-pocked stone a meaning past
the blurred engraving of the fibrous frost.

So I, because of all the buried men
in Ulster clay, because of rock and glen
and mist and cloud and quality of air
as Irish in my thought as any here,
who now would make a rime to fix that thought
in pauper speech stand mouthing all my doubt,
and have no skill in either mode of song,
the graver English, or lyric Irish tongue.

VALENTIN IREMONGER

ELIZABETH

Elizabeth, frigidly stretched,
On a spring day surprised us
With her starched dignity and the quietness
Of her hands clasping a black cross.

With book and candle and holy-water dish
She received us in the room with the blind down.
Her eyes were peculiarly closed and we knelt shyly
Noticing the blot of her hair on the white pillow.

We met that evening by the crumbling wall
In the field behind the house where I lived
And talked it over but could find no reason
Why she had left us whom she had liked so much.

Death, yes, we understood: something to do
With age and decay, decrepit bodies.
But here was this vigorous one, aloof and prim
Who would not answer our furtive whispers.

Next morning, hearing the priest call her name,
I fled outside, being full of certainty,
And cried my seven years against the church's stone wall.
For eighteen years I did not speak her name

Until this autumn day when, in a gale,
A sapling fell outside my window, its branches
Rebelliously blotting the lawn's green. Suddenly, I thought
Of Elizabeth, frigidly stretched.

IN NEW ROSS

In this quiet town, it is odd to discover
A day buried so deeply in the debris of years
And to dig it out, not damaged at all, discoloured
With dust to be wiped away like tears.
Why here, of all places? Was it the fall
Of sunlight on the trees beyond or the startling call
Of a trumpet unexpectedly down the street, lay
Flush with the memory and pathos of that day?

Say, anyhow, it was: for love like trumpets then
Shattered the walls of our reserve in a sunlit garden
When, over the hedge, you threw the cherries to me and again
Innocence gave us a blessing and a pardon
As little we thought of the fleet, disturbing swallow
Along airlines in the garden skidding, stuttering its warning
Of night over the horizon implacably throbbing
With answers both for our laughing and our sobbing.

O Elizabeth, the gold trumpets no more
Curl for you their notes, though the cherry-tree
Each year displays its wares in hope
Your fingers will fondle them caressingly:
And here is my youth, like a bright ribbon, soiled
By death, my days, the dustbin gang, the broken delph, destroyed
By hopes that leave like visitors and leave
A trail of stains that smiling won't conceal.

Yet now, watching the swallows bank over the trees
There where the river bends, suddenly I find time to wonder
What can stop the cough in my life or ease
The choking effects of so many blunders—
Somewhere there should be love aloud like music.
Over the hunching hills, the wires go trailing their furious
Messages, the oiled machinery of nature shunts
Day down for repairs. Silently, the night's technicians hunt.

THESE APPLE TREES

These apple-trees shall be resplendent again
In their pearl-draped vanity, when summer smacks hard
Home in the next year, playing its trump card
After winter's gamble and the spring's slick stratagem.
These bushes, too, the berry and the currant,
Shall swank it through the autumn in their new rig-out,
Swaying their laden shoulders with the seductive, insolent
Assurance of girls in evening dress dining out.

Who would have the heart to speak then of decline?
Not I, nor Elizabeth; although each new summer
For us is not a period of festival, of drumming
Blood flowering and shooting a line
But another warped and rusted leaf to cover
The rich earth of our youth and our horn-mad days
When every note of the clock brought us another lover
Each, and another love-song to phrase.

Now while winter strikes its first-round gong
Bringing all the dryads, crying, from the woods,
If you look carefully, you will see the buds
Curl up snugly in their own warmth.
Already they plan dresses, make their dates, decide
The menus for their roaring parties, engage
The bands that will provide both sweet and jive
When light-fingered spring flicks over another page.

But from me, in this garden, confidence slips like a shawl,
Watching the leaves like damaged gliders toss
And tailspin in the southern warm wind and cut across
The path, between her and the low granite wall,
Knowing the infective evil latent
In their rust, how the disease, contracted, spreads,
The limbs, once cramped, never to be again straightened,
Or summer detonate in our heads.

EVENING IN SUMMER

All evening, while the summer trees were crying
Their sudden realisation of the spring's sad death,
Somewhere a clock was ticking and we heard it here
In the sun-porch, where we sat so long, buying
Thoughts for a penny from each other. Near
Enough it was and loud to make us talk beneath our breath.

And a time for quiet talking it was, to be sure, although
The rain would have drowned the sound of our combined voices.
The spring of our youth that night suddenly dried
And summer filled the veins of our lives like slow
Water into creeks edging. Like the trees you cried.
Autumn and winter, you said, had so many disguises

And how could we be always on the watch to plot
A true perspective for each minute's value. I couldn't reply,
So many of my days toppled into the past unnoticed.
Silence like sorrow multiplied around you, a lot
Of whose days counted so much. My heart revolted
That time for you should be such a treacherous ally,

And though, midnight inclining bells over the city
With a shower of sound like tambourines of Spain
Gay in the teeth of the night air, I thought
Of a man who said the truth was in the pity,
Somehow, under the night's punched curtain, I was lost.
I only knew the pity and the pain.

GOING DOWN THE MOUNTAIN

"I'm going down," she said, tying her yellow scarf,
While I still watched the dull grey mountain road
Mooch down into the glen and disappear
Round a curve of trees and cottages. Some sudden fear
Made me not reply, or make any attempt to start
Yet awhile; I sat on the old sacrificial stone

To which we had climbed all the hot morning together,
Choosing the difficult way, along the dried-up river bed
Choked with dead boulders covered with a fur of spruce leaves.
Not even the sacrifice of our youth—made at noon—redeems
The swinging boughs of our minds, gay with feathers,
Lopped from us now. "I'm going down," she said.

Her teeth were hedges of dense white sloe-blossom,
Her hair a development of black. Down the afternoon
From the rare peak of youth, too, we are going to the valley
Of age, lurching and stumbling down its gothic alleys
And grotesque approaches. "I'm going down." The gossip
Of the wind in her hair will be stopped much too soon.

HECTOR

Talking to her, he knew it was the end,
The last time he'd speed her into sleep with kisses:
Achilles had it in for him and was fighting mad.
The roads of his longing she again wandered,
A girl desirable as midsummer's day.

He was a marked man and he knew it,
Being no match for Achilles whom the gods were backing.
Sadly he spoke to her for hours, his heart
Snapping like sticks, she on his shoulder crying.
Yet, sorry only that the meaning eluded him,

He slept well all night, having caressed
Andromache like a flower, though in a dream he saw
A body lying on the sands, huddled and bleeding,
Near the feet a sword in bits and by the head,
An upturned, dented helmet.

THE DOG

All day the unnatural barking of dogs
Sounded in my ears. In O'Connell Street, among the crowd,
A dog barked at my heels but, when I looked, was gone.
Sitting at my window, later, at nearly three o'clock,
Glad for the quiet harmony of the afternoon,
A voice reached up like a long arm out of the street
To rap on the shutters of my ears but when I looked
The street's chaste line was unbroken, its perspective unstained.

Now, lying awake in bed, smoking,
Looking out the window, I can see him,
Lean-faced and shaggy, as the moonlight falls
Sideways into my room as into a chapel,
Where he squats on the lawn, tilting his lonely snout,
Raising his lost unnatural cry.

God send his master is not dead or none he loves
Being out of countenance has sent him for succour
And that I don't understand his plaintiveness:
But yet, God help me, I fear this unnatural barking
Has something to do with me and not with strangers
As quietly I lie, hearing the hours tick by
And the unsatisfied dog howling upon the lawn,
Breaking the night's maidenhead.

IN THIS RIVER

In this river, flooded by recent rains,
The current sobs heavily like a girl
Watching her day angrily warp and curl
Into scales of white foam like a dragon's mail.
Danger is on tap like oil, insolent, yet all
The olive-green pike, the brilliant-finned perch, behind the wall
Of weeds, where the shallows were, can cower
Grimly, counting their safety out hour by hour.

Looking across the garden towards the river, alone, I think
How, for us, flooded by circumstance, no weedy margins
Offer their dubious protection as we stand, uncertain,
With our hands hanging, by winter's brink,
Yet ours, all spring and summer, was the screwed concentration
On crops and fuel, preparing for this evil season,
Neither birds nor flowers tempting our attention, nor even
Gay girls laughing in the hay-meadows, wheedling.

Silently, in late November, we in this soured land
Wait the Hunger Moon, the days closing in, rain
Gunning the windows, the wind rising, the pain
Of winter already in our numbed hands.
How will we live for the next twelve months
Is the bare question, seeing the results
Of our years' labours, turf-clamps ruined, the tempting
Harvest lost, and all our store-houses empty.

ICARUS

As, even today, the airman, feeling the plane sweat
Suddenly, seeing the horizon tilt up gravely, the wings shiver,
Knows that, for once, Daedalus has slipped up badly,
Drunk on the job, perhaps, more likely dreaming, high-flier Icarus,
Head butting down, skidding along the light-shafts
Back, over the tones of the sea-waves and the slipstream, heard
The gravel-voiced, stuttering trumpets of his heart

Sennet among the crumbling court-yards of his brain the mistake
Of trusting somebody else in an important affair like this;
And, while the flat sea, approaching, buckled into oh! avenues
Of acclamation, he saw the wrong story fan out into history,
Truth, undefined, lost in his own neglect. On the hills,
The summer-shackled hills, the sun spanged all day;
Love and the world were young and there was no ending:

But star-chaser, big-time-going, chancer Icarus
Like a dog on the sea lay and the girls forgot him
And Daedalus, too busy hammering another job,
Remembered him only in pubs. No bugler at all
Sobbed taps for the young fool then, reported missing,
Presumed drowned, wing-bones and feathers on the tides
Drifting in casually, one by one.

MY SUBTLE
AND PROCLAMANT SONG

Our tears have fallen for this world of stone:
these wrinkled rocks have wept, yes even these
that bubbled out under a glaring sun
for these cold islands in the desolate seas.

Time lifted to the gape of the dead moon
draws in his lines among the water weeds
and weeps for us: the weak and rebel man
who cries defiance in the child he breeds,

and, breathing smoke along the level air
of winter, works out his sin of pride
without repentance, that no god shall dare
to drive his anger through the dusty shroud.

Yet in this unborn infant shall I live
through following time, who bend the knee to death,
and flatter nothing that, even in love,
the carious bone shall be my monolith.

For this soft child shall in my rotting years
through his wild reins adventure for new worlds,
command what has escaped me in the weirs
of inviolable time, the treasures of shells.

His flesh shall be my stone, the word he speaks
with no matter how uncaring tongue
my epitaph; his living hours and weeks
my subtle and proclamant song.

103

OLD JOYCE

I am broken by the tumult of the years:
on me they bend the fury of their anger,
the iron of their hate. I have watched them,
watched them rise and have their flood of summer,
and watched them fall through the dry autumn evil
and lie among the slush and sludge of winter,
the dead end of time. And I have wept
because they passed so quickly, wept although
not one but brought me agony and shame,
not one but brought me loss and bitterness,
failure and humiliation. I remember
how one girl turned her back, and how another
mocked me for the thinness of my wrist,
or perhaps because I would not join the dance.
I had some other things to think of.
And men talked of me, and at times despised me,
and I have never understood. Their laughter
was not my way, nor did I hope for it.
To-morrow was my constant care. My plans
were all built on the promise of to-morrow,
and I looked forward to my constant dawn.

Even the dead are not so lonely at heart
as I am guarded by these eighty years.

I grow too old now for a fresh endeavour.
My youth lies under the rubble of my days,
and it was never eager. Security
was what I wanted. Now it locks my limbs
in strict propriety; and cumulative custom
imposes barrenness and impotence.
Even the dead are not so poor of heart
as I the heir of all my eighty years.

Sometimes I think I am the lusty lion,
sometimes the agile rabbit in the meadow,
sometimes the bird whose note shakes all the wood:

TURF-MAN

but this old mummy fails, these stiffened limbs,
this shrivelled fist of heart, my scroggle pipe,
even desire. I might have played the lover once,
have played it all, and with success
have forced a sweet surrender.
It is too late.

These eighty counters, all the wage I won,
I wish that I could drop them in a cap
close by some barbarous scrawl,
or in a blind man's cup.

MERCHANDISE

Driving down from the turf bog in the rain
he saw the broad boats drawn up on the strand
and the queer dark men who, ankle deep
in water, humped their bales on to the land,

and lashed his ass all down the mountain road
and offered turf for barter, turf to pay
for silk and wine; but those dark men
looked at his load and laughed, and turned away.

THE ISLAND

This island is the world's end. Beyond
the wide Atlantic drives its thunderous tides
backwards and forwards, beating on the land,
time out of mind, a hammer on the heart,
and the storms of the west race from the huge
infinity of sea, gathering anger,
and split their bellies and their fist of rage
against the island's shattered silent mountain.

The puffins and the rabbits own the land
and the gull and the circling ravenous eagle
and the seals bark on the edge of the sound
between the black rocks where the sea beats.
Where men trod once and wore the hard earth bare
the green illimitable grass
creeps back, over the garden and the gear
that fished the sea and farmed the ungenerous soil.

A lizard by a loosened door
peers into an abandoned room,
twisting his nostrils to the mummied air
that bore the shape of words, a cradle tale,
or some young girl's fresh, careless, idle song:
the sea wind and the subtle rain
break down all things at last, even the strong
stone of the wall, and the stubborn heart.

And yet they loved this island. Its hard rock
became their bone, its meagre earth their flesh,
the sea their tide of blood; and in the black
night they turned its sullenness to song.
The dancing foot that stirred the scattered sand
is quiet now or heavy overseas
and the singing voice has only songs that wound
with bitterness. The land is dead.

MAHONEY

Then Mahoney, standing in the surf,
the convoy hanging in the misty sea
and landing forces moving up the beach,
dropped down his arms, and said
I wait, O God, I wait,
and these were his last words of common speech.

Christ in the shallows of the water walked
or in the sweaty hollow of his palm

appeared and spoke to his reluctant bone
or moved about the chambers of his skull,
the scourger of the temple, with a whip;
and in his heart also the lash had been.

So Mahoney stood and let his rifle fall
into the sea, where lug-worms claimed it, and
the servant tide; and heard his captain shout,
but did not move; and felt the weight of wheels
and tracks across the cortex of his brain;
but did not certainly hear the single shot.

Wife, children, parents, weep for him, who now
dead with the grey crabs and the starfish rests
where surges heap on him the slow and secret sand.
Yet even in the valleys of the sea
the dead can feel the libel, and Mahoney
in his stripped skull is tortured by a lie.

OMPHALOS: THE WELL

I

By hard journeys in a dead land
that arid summer fills with bitter fire
or brittle winter
broods blue and bright as glass on;
by hard journeys through broken cities
in bleak day or black night
in sultry light or suffocating dark
in circumstance of four seasons
expected and repetitive:
I come at last
weary and easeless and without wonder
and with no sure relief
to a well of sweet water
and find there kites and vultures.

I have need of the water
I am avid of the water
after that journey in the dry land
where at each step
the tongueless dusts of the dead
rose like ghosts to seize
and silence the living tongue
and heap their drifts within the beating heart.

II

I cried aloud in the wilderness
where no man heard
over the round eye of the well
over the ashes of the dead:
See, O see, I have come at last
where you have long expected me.
Do you not know me
by the sweet water of life,
by the holy omphalos?

Give me leave to drink.

No man heard
but the ashes lifted before my breath
and hid the sun
and polluted the water of the well.

In violence of anger
I broke the well:
and let loose the water
over the land
and the land burst into leaf
and the leaf into flower
and the flower into fruit.

III

The silent scavengers
lifted their heads
and spread their huge black wings
and flew across the land
with famine in their beaks
because a cracked old voice
chanted a ranting tune
that made the living heart
a servant of death.

Black the land and black the broken stone
and black the splintered butt of the tree
and black the burned bone and the rotten flesh:
layer over layer ashes cloak the earth
where late the green tree stood
or great cities proclaimed the power of men:
black the hollow embers of thought
and black the cinders of faith:
all burned and bared to the bone.

IV

Is there hope
in annihilation?
Is there pity
in death?
Is there life
beyond despair?

The hard journey in the dead land
is to do again. Weariness and despair
benumb the soil, but the end remains:
the water of the well is always sweet;
the sap that swells the bud in the black branch
and the thrust of blood in the limb
continue, a strong river,
beyond the end of our understanding.

AN UPPER ROOM

(In any town of the world where patriots have striven)

The noises of the street come up subdued,
And in some curious blend that has a new
Strange meaning in the mumbled many-hued
Soft spoken ghosts of words that have passed through
The talk of other generations gone before,
Until, it seems, one might push in my door
And say, 'I fought in such a year, but you forgot.
This house, this street, this town would flourish not
For you today if I had never been,
If I had never seen what I have seen.'
And as the door shuts out again the street
Hums with its mumbling noises from below
Where still those generations, to and fro,
Mysteriously greet.

FOR C.K.

At His Christening

We wish to the new child
A heart that can be beguiled
By a flower
That the wind lifts
As he passes,
By the light that is on the grasses
After a summer shower;
A heart that can recognize,
Without aid of the eyes,
The gifts
That life holds for the wise.

111

If the storms break for him,
May the trees shake for him
Their blossoms down!
In the night that he is troubled
May a friend wake for him
So that his time be doubled!
And at the end
Of all loving and love,
May the Man above
Give him a crown!

ITS NAME IS KNOWN

There is bright light
In the depth of rivers, even at night;
In the glossy sides
Of stone that leans on stone
In the still water it abides:
At a wind breaking down hunted from the sky
Through the stirred water, it will blink an eye.

The heart that is the hunted wind
Has skill to find
It, every place.
The finding can atone
For all the torture of the chase.
Its name is known;
Some call it love, some grace.

MOTHER

I have lost her, I know;
But she is with me still, wherever I go,
    In thought or in dream,
    Like the gleam
Of a silvery evening shut in a little pool

That a child sees, and he coming from school
With a primrose in his hand,
    And he swinging it left and right
In a way you would never understand,
    Unless you could see with that other sight
The skilled musicians there,
Around him in the nimble air.

TO THE SPRING SUN

Unplait the braided dark
Of winter days; unstall
The bright-hoofed waterfall.
And with bold glance lay bare
The yellow tigers ambushed in the hair.

Through leaf-deserted park
And besomed field, now leash
The cymbal winds that clash.
And with kind fingers pull
From jerkined buds their undervests of wool.

Implant in thrush and lark
The seed of light, so they
Shall start their roundelay,
And every tree unglove
That all its folded hands may stretch with love.

AT THE PARTY

Amber the wine.
Voices like candles shine.
But I can hear,
Like hollow seas, upon some inner ear

Pounding, a bell
Distant and lonely toll
Darkly. For whom?
Who travels this night sightless to his tomb?

A nameless one
Who bears upon his bone

Imprint of woe,
All naked unutterable sorrow,

As black a grief
As boughs bereaved of leaf,
And as tearless
As the skies above dry deserts' bareness.

All sadness lies
Upon his shuttered eyes,
As in the tomb
Sinks he for whom earth's tree has shed its bloom.

Bring in more wine
That voices still may shine
And I alone
Hear candle-voices waver as they burn.

WHEN FROM THE CALYX-CANOPY OF NIGHT

When from the calyx-canopy of night
The flower of our loveliness unsheathed,
Under the black dew of the darkest hour
The earth dissolved, and everything was void
But this flower's chalice.

Then did the tendrils of my ultimate spirit,
Reaching out delicate antennae, so to seek
You and be known of you, discover
The inconceivable answer to the unframed question.

And when the petals of the hour of love
Folded to a dove's nest in the feathered dark
Pinioned with silence, and great continents
Rose slowly from penumbral seas of dream,
Then as one dove we soared, and took our flight
Across their shadowy forests into sleep.

WHEN TO MY SERENE BODY

When to my serene body yours
Leans in a quiet ecstasy
And coolly our limbs
Seek their several felicity,
The skin with its silken kiss
Moves creamily over skin
Into a dream that is
A tower of the skin's thought;
Your body melting to mine,
Cool and warm at once,
And water-smooth, in the sun's
Long amorous ardour caught.

Its own need pursuing,
Skin, the body's dress,
In a separate loveliness,
Along belly and thigh and breast,
Sinks in its long caress.

THE BULL

'I am an urn of anger,' cried the bull,
'A Hecla of ebullient peppercorns.
Dislike rings all the gongs upon my hoofs
And shakes the sharp dilemma of my horns.

So let me run in gyres to the North,
And steep in the alembic of the snows
My acrimonious hoofs, till they release
Their flowers of anger, rose on waspish rose.

And where the circular turnstile of the Pole
Takes toll from nights but hardly any morns,
I'll pluck at last the black choleric fruit
That ripens on the branches of my horns.'

THE WELCOME

Awaits no solar quadriga,
But a musty cab,
Whose wheels' revolving spiders scare
Pigeons from plump pavanes among the cobbles.

Past the green and yellow grins
Of bold advertisements
On the walls of the Temple of Arrival and Departure,
(Due homage to the puffing goddesses,

Stout, butting with iron bosoms),
We drive, and watch
The geometry of the Dublin houses
Circle and square themselves; march orderly;

Past the waterfalls of lace dripping
Elegantly in tall windows;
Under a sun oblique above the streets'
Ravines; and past the river,

Like the slippery eel of Time,
Eluding us; eight miles clopping
Behind the horse's rump to where
The mouth of Dublin gulps at the sea.

And there beside the harbour
And the castle,
And the yellow rocks and the black-backed gulls,
The piebald oyster-catchers, limpets, lobster-pots,

There is a house with a child in it,
Two cats like ebony
(Or liquorice); and a kitten with a face
Like a black pansy, a bunch of fronded paws;

And a dog brighter than a new chestnut,—
A house with a bed

Like an emperor's in it,—
It is late. Let us pay the cabman and go in.

Here we shall run up the spiral staircase
Of our laughter.
We shall be no older
Than the child and the animals.

VIATICUM

The sluice gates of sleep are open wide
and through the House its soothing silver tide
from ward to ward flows grave and deep;
now flood, now fretful trickle,
and some it leaves marooned
who cannot sleep.
The nurses chart its course all night
and those who drowse and those who tell their beads
and those who coma vigil keep.
Sunken beyond the lure of light
some watch the shadows with unfocused eyes,
dull and indifferent, ears attuned
to soundless music of the Boatman's oar
and rhythmic singing of the rowlocks' strain
as the dark ferry swings to shore.
An old old woman and a little child
soon will meet each other there
but who knows what gay roisterer
before this dawn will pay their fare.

INSOMNIA

Tell them to go away:
last night Cuchulain slammed the gate five times
and hammered on the window panes,
and then his dog sat on the lawn
and howled and whined,
and after that a beggar banshee keened
and put the Ulster hound to shame.
I have not slept.
Then towards the dawn
strange workmen flickered saffron flags of flame

startling the shadows from their secret raths
to leap and bound about the walls,
and doffed the candle's silken hood,
the wick bereft was blunt and blackened as a clove.
They tapped and tinkered on the frozen pipes,
I heard their creak upon the cistern stairs
till in the peevish light
the clangour of the convent bell
like a ship staggering through clammy fog,
banished all phantoms and I slept.
Tell them to go away till noon
and I will bind in dreams the wraiths
that pilfered last night's sleep.

GHOSTS

A ripple of dust panicked across
a busy street
timidly darting through horses' feet
and I saw a well beloved ghost
walk haltingly up
to the Provost's house.
But I was not near
and in a daze
watched the dust dwindle and disappear
and the light grow bleak
from the muffled skies
battening down hope
on my famished eyes.
What do they seek
so patiently?
Have we broken trust
that they turn away
and never speak,
or must
our parched eyes
endless aspergillum play
to lay this cold and lovely dust?

A REVEL

I'd fill up the house with guests this minute
And have them drinking in every room
And the laughter wrecking the garden quiet.
Citymen dressed in a sober style
Who never soiled a buckled shoe,
And wild country boys with a frieze coat flapping
That were never within an ass's roar
Of a city street, and shining girls
In every fashion. I'd call them in
Out of every year for the past ten hundred
And make them safe at their own table,
The men whose blood is safe in my veins.

I'd have no aged ghosts struggling out of the grave,
But lively lads that I'd borrow from time,
And till Peter's bird set them screaming homeward
The neighbours hearing that heady laughter
Would think it a wedding or a wake.

I'd leave uncertain the hour of departure,
But while night was pasted black on the windows
We'd talk of love, and blood to blood
We'd speak one language; tinker and poet,
The tramps who were hurled from their own possessions
And the wealthy men would talk flesh to flesh,
The years dissolved that were huge between them.

And one would tell of the time of hunger,
The mouths stained green in a ditch's end,
Earth cleared for action and hunger rearing
High in the belly, a country withered
Before Spring's rally. But another would shout
Of a night of drinking, the senses loosed
And the traces broken
And the drink as mild as the milky way.

Fathers would lean on their grandsons' shoulders
And great-great-grandsons pass a glass
And laugh in the face of their great-grandfather;
And together we'd find the spirit within us
Too wild to be bound by house or wall,
And only the dawn and the cock's alarm
Could save the town. Then home they'd rush
Hot in their leather.

Heir to them all
I'd count them over, recall the nose
And the curve of the mouth, till sleep would slip
Through the wakening window and curl about me,
And I, like them, would be lost in time.

THE HUNGRY GRASS

Crossing the shallow holdings high above sea
Where few birds nest, the luckless foot may pass
From the bright safety of experience
Into the terror of the hungry grass.

Here in a year when poison from the air
First withered in despair the growth of spring
Some skull-faced wretch whom nettle could not save
Crept on four bones to his last scattering;

Crept, and the shrivelled heart which drove his thought
Towards platters brought in hospitality
Burst as the wizened eyes measured the miles
Like dizzy walls forbidding him the city.

Little the earth reclaimed from that poor body;
And yet, remembering him, the place has grown
Bewitched, and the thin grass he nourishes
Racks with his famine, sucks marrow from the bone.

CONNEMARA COLLEEN

PROTHALAMIUM

And so must I lose her whose mind
Fitted so sweetly and securely into mine
That words seeded and blossomed in an instant,
Whose body was one of my fine
Morning visions come alive and perfect?
Must she slip out of my arms so
And I never revel again in the twilight of her hair
Or see the world grow
Marvellous within her eye? My hands
Are empty; and suddenly I think
That on some night like this, when rain is soft
And moths flutter at the window, seeking a chink,
I'll lose her utterly, a bedded bride
Gold ring and contract bound,
The night filled with terrifying music
And she not hearing a sound.

LOVE'S LANGUAGE

As to a sacrament
Quiet I go,
Desiring no gay words
No carnival show.

A wordless communion
Of lip upon lip,
Passionate language
Of swift finger tip

These are my sayings.
Silence and night
Veil from our eyes that
Time is in flight.

CHILDHOOD

The Lord frowned down from every wall,
Saint Patrick with his mitred head
Exorcised the evil worm,
Saint John surveyed the brass-bound bed

Which jingled like a Christmas sleigh.
A shrieking woman tore his will,
Rending the flesh with savage nails
And eyes that had the greed to kill.

The haggard face and naked eyes
Harassed his senses. Saint Joseph smiled
Upon the violence and the calm,
Holding the lily and the Child.

THE WIND BLOWS

There's little wildness in my city head
Except when wind and rain tear off the lid
And blow among the passions lying hid—

Then all my thoughts go wild, go gay, the red
Roaring stranger in the house breaks out
And every gentle guests's a ranting lout

Dancing the naked hillsides in the rain
With young girls in the glitter of their youth
Whose bodies are their beauty and their truth.

But soon the shivered clouds are sealed again,
The wind goes belling into another chase—
I fail for breath and cannot keep that pace.

GALWAY

Galway called out of sleep
And wakened the port of the mind
And the islands that crouch on the water
Hiding under the wind
Sailed up properly
Boats and gulls and turf-smoke
And a cliff high as Nelson
Called till I woke
And cast all the symbols away
And thought of the Corrib in flood,
Rain hammering on the brain
A town moored in mud.

DUBLIN MADE ME

Dublin made me and no little town
With the country closing in on its streets,
The cattle walking proudly on its pavements,
The jobbers, the gombeenmen and the cheats

Devouring the Fair Day between them,
A public-house to half a hundred men,
And the teacher, the solicitor and the bank-clerk
In the hotel bar, drinking for ten.

Dublin made me, not the secret poteen still,
The raw and hungry hills of the West,
The lean road flung over profitless bog
Where only a snipe could nest,

Where the sea takes its tithe of every boat.
Bawneen and curragh have no allegiance of mine,
Nor the cute, self-deceiving talkers of the South
Who look to the East for a sign.

The soft and dreary midlands with their tame canals
Wallow between sea and sea, remote from adventure,
And Northward a far and fortified province
Crouches under the lash of arid censure.

I disclaim all fertile meadows, all tilled land,
The evil that grows from it, and the good,
But the Dublin of old statutes, this arrogant city,
Stirs proudly and secretly in my blood.

GOING TO MASS LAST SUNDAY

(*Tune:* The Lowlands of Holland)

Going to Mass last Sunday my true love passed me by,
I knew her mind was altered by the rolling of her eye;
And when I stood in God's dark light my tongue could word no
     prayer
Knowing my saint had fled and left her reliquary bare.

Sweet faces smiled from holy glass, demure in saintly love,
Sweet voices ripe with Latin grace rolled from the choir above;
But brown eyes under Sunday wear were all my liturgy;
How can she hope for heaven who has so deluded me?

When daffodils were altar gold her lips were light on mine
And when the hawthorn flame was bright we drank the year's new
     wine;
The nights seemed stained-glass windows lit with love that paled
     the sky,
But love's last ember perishes in the winter of her eye.

Drape every downcast day now in purple cloth of Lent,
Smudge every forehead now with ash, that she may yet repent,
Who going to Mass last Sunday could pass so proudly by
And show her mind was altered by the rolling of an eye.

DODONA'S OAKS WERE STILL

He told the barmaid he had things to do,
Such as to find out what we are and why.
He said, I must have winter in the mountains;
Spring is no good, nor summer,
And even autumn carries too much colour.
I must have winter. Winter's naked line
Is truth revealed and there's a discipline
Along the edges of gaunt rocks on frosty nights.
She said she thought so too,
And so he left
Bookshops and music and the sight of friends,
Good smokeroom laughter starred with epigrams,
Seven sweet bridges and those bucking trams
That blunder west through bitter history,—
And women,
Perhaps particularly women,
Climbing like slow white maggots through his thought;
He left the lot,
And got him to a shack above the city,
Lit a white candle to his solitude
And searched among the images he'd seen
Of his own self in other minds to find
Mankind in him.
He hoped to see the whole
Diverse and complicated world
Fold up and pack itself into his soul
The way a walnut's packed.
The lonely fool,
Squatting among the heavy mountain shapes,
Looked on the wet black branches and the red,
Followed the urgent branches to their tips
And back again through twig and stem to root,
Always alone and busy with himself,
Enquiring if this world of decent men

Must be hell's kitchen to the end of time,
Because of that old sin, intolerable pride,
Strong powers of angels soured by impotence,
Rebellious godhead working its hot way
Through tangled veins.
He cried in pain towards the writhing trees,
But heard no voice.
Dodona's oaks were still.

THIS MORNING I WAKENED AMONG LOUD CRIES
OF SEAGULLS

This morning I wakened among loud cries of seagulls
Thronging in misty light above my neighbour's ploughland,
And the house in its solid acres was carried wheeling
Encircled in desolate waters and impenetrable cloudy
Wet winds that harried and lost the sea-bird's voices
And the voice of my darling, despairing and drowning,
Lost beyond finding in the bodiless poising
Dissolving shapes of grey mist crowding,
Till the wind grew still and the water noiseless.

Later, when the sun groped down and flung wide open
Mist-hung curtains from laughing brilliant meadows,
Taking my rod I crossed by grassy slopes
To the sunshot river and fished a run of shadows,
But between each take and strike her nervous fingers lightly
Twitched my tense elbow and I missed him, turning
To that beloved face,—but, oh sweet Christ,
The shining air was empty! And choked with earth
And roots of grass I gnawed the day to twilight.

Big-boned and breasted like her own timeless mountains
She broke herself to housecraft, groping in crowded shadows,
Nursing a brood of phantoms until her days were shrouded
From warmth of sun or love or help of kindly hands,—
And oh white fog had clouded the valleys when I rose,

Had scarfed the water's face and choked the source of twilight;
Owl-hoot and chuck of water-fowl came dropping ghostly
Passing wan hosts of jonquils in the wood where silence
Gathered the grey trunks as I stumbled homeward.

BE STILL AS YOU ARE BEAUTIFUL

Be still as you are beautiful,
    Be silent as the rose;
Through miles of starlit countryside
    Unspoken worship flows
To reach you in your loveless room
    From lonely men whom daylight gave
The blessing of your passing face
    Impenetrably grave.

A white owl in the lichened wood
    Is circling silently;
More secret and more silent yet
    Must be your love to me.
Thus, while about my dreaming head
    Your soul in ceaseless vigil goes,
Be still as you are beautiful,
    Be silent as the rose.

THE RIVER

Stir not, whisper not,
Trouble not the giver
Of quiet who gives
This calm-flowing river,

Whose whispering willows,
Whose murmuring reeds
Make silence more still
Than the thought it breeds,

Until thought drops down
From the motionless mind
Like a quiet brown leaf
Without any wind;

It falls on the river
And floats with its flowing,
Unhurrying still
Past caring, past knowing.

Ask not, answer not,
Trouble not the giver
Of quiet who gives
This calm-flowing river.

WAKING

Peace, there is peace in this awaking.
Slowly, silently the warm sun
Enters my being, waves are breaking
Unseen as time, one after one
Endlessly breaking. A seagull crying
Voices eternity. There stirs
A wind among the grass and, sighing,
Carries my spirit to hers.

THE SNARE

He stoops above the clumsy snare
To take the night's yet living loot,
When the wild creature kicking there
Beside the thorn-tree's tunnelled root,
Flings up red soil into his eyes—
And suddenly the April skies
Are loud with pain of man and brute,
Until he lifts a clabbered boot

And stamps red life into the sod,
And silence takes the fields again—
The old deceptive peace of God!

SONG

She spoke to me gently with words of sweet meaning,
    Like the damsel was leaning on Heaven's half-door,
And her bright eyes besought me to leave off deceiving
    And trouble the parish with scandal no more.

And there, for a moment, I thought I'd be better
    To take those round arms for a halter and live
Secure and respectable, safe in her shelter,
    And be the bright pattern of boys in the village.

But I thought how the lane would have sheltering shadows
    And a glass on the counter would look as before;
And the house was too dark, and her eyes were too narrow,
    So I left her alone at her door.

SHE WALKED UNAWARE

O, she walked unaware of her own increasing beauty
That was holding men's thoughts from market or plough,
 As she passed by, intent on her womanly duties,
And she without leisure to be wayward or proud;
Or if she had pride then it was not in her thinking
But thoughtless in her body like a flower of good breeding.
The first time I saw her spreading coloured linen
 Beyond the green willow she gave me gentle greeting
With no more intention than the leaning willow tree.

Though she smiled without intention yet from that day forward
Her beauty filled like water the four corners of my being,
And she rested in my heart like a hare in the form

That is shaped to herself. And I that would be singing
 Or whistling at all times went silently then;
Till I drew her aside among straight stems of beeches
When the blackbird was sleeping and she promised that never
The fields would be ripe but I'd gather all sweetness,
A red moon of August would rise on our wedding.

October is spreading bright flame along stripped willows,
Low fires of the dogwood burn down to grey water—
God pity me now and all desolate sinners
Demented with beauty! I have blackened my thought
In drouths of bad longing, and all brightness goes shrouded
Since he came with his rapture of wild words that mirrored
Her beauty and made her ungentle and proud.
To-night she will spread her brown hair on his pillow,
But I shall be hearing the harsh cries of wild fowl.

THE WIDOW OF DRYNAM

I stand in my door and look over the low field of Drynam.
No man but the one man has known me, no child but the one
Grew big at my breast, and what are my sorrows beside
That pride and that glory? I come from devotions on Sunday
And leave them to pity or spite; and though I who had music have
     none
But crying of seagulls at morning and calling of curlews at night,
I wake and remember my beauty and think of my son
Who would stare the loud fools into silence
And rip the dull parish asunder.

Small wonder indeed he was wild with breeding and beauty
And why would my proud lad not straighten his back from the
     plough?
My son was not got and I bound in a cold bed of duty
Nor led to the side of the road by some clay-clabbered lout!
No, but rapt by a passionate poet away from the dancers
To curtains and silver and firelight,—
O wisely and gently he drew down the pale shell of satin

And all the bright evening's adornment and clad me
Again in the garment of glory, the joy of his eyes.

I stand in my door and look over the low fields of Drynam
When skies move westward, the way he will come from the war;
Maybe on a morning of March when a thin sun is shining
And starlings have blackened the thorn,
He will come, my bright limb of glory, my mettlesome wild one,
With coin in his pocket and tales on the tip of his tongue,
And the proud ones that slight me will bring back forgotten
    politeness
To see me abroad on the roads with my son,
The two of us laughing together or stepping in silence.

WILLIAM BLAKE SEES GOD

The cool sky opens like a hand,
Widening into a wound,
A mouth of song. Coldly they stand,
The precise angels, pruned
To leaf-light singing. William Blake
Lifts his face to God.
But the light leaves of singing break
And he turns thickly, shod
With unbelief, uneasily
Feeling the question-mark
Rear and snarl on him inwardly,
The strangler in the dark.

ELEGY

Out on the roads of sky the moon stands poised
Like some pale traveller, hand raised at door.
The fields turn, mouthing incoherent cries,
And the hills are gentle, kneeling by the shore.
Yes, he is one with them, being underground.
His eyes are in the water, his grey hands
Part the limp leaves; and his throat is swollen full
With the song of the last bird, a broken sound
Like weeping of hidden women heard at night
When stars are stones and small winds congregate:
He has returned to life. O look, he lies
Cold in the shallows of the ebbing light,
A tree grown through his heart. He has become
Great with the soil, and holds converse with God,
Who is a tree rearing through his heart
And the red clay drawing his body home.

AN AGED WRITER

I

He would burn his books and gladly die
If, levelling those walls that hem his mind,
He, mountain-shouldered, sky-proud, could with eye
Moon-raised unmask time's metaphors and find
The naked features of eternity.

To break or blend with time? The question ran
Grooving his years till, grieving, he discerned
No answer waited for the dying man.
Now, spurning thought, the icy mind has turned
For alms from heaven, bread conjured from stone.

II

I would tell you if I knew.
The gull signs the air, but you
Watch at windows wondering
What mystery conceived the wing.

I would break the clouds and show
The circle's face, the ebb and flow
Of time and that eternity
Which gnaws and nags at you and me.

I would make your death a song
Of meaning, old man, with a throng
Of explanations round your bed.
O I would ease your haunted head.

The gull signs the air; and you
Brood upon those cherished few
Words you culled from mystery.
Now let them be your elegy.

THE WHITE BIRD

I made a loaf of bread
And scattered it in crumbs
Under the yellowing tree,
For the white bird with the red
Beak and glittering eyes,
Who sits indifferently
Turning a cold white head.

I culled old recipes
And made a loaf of bread
And scattered every crumb
Under the yellowing trees;
But he humps stony wings:
Pickpocket starlings come;
The quiet rat pillages.

If I could lay a hand
Upon that cold white head
And plumb those glittering eyes
And come to understand
That unrelenting beak,
I'd silence all those cries
That desolate the land.

EPITHALAMIUM

So you are married, girl. It makes me sad,
Somehow, to think of that: that you, once held
Between hot hands on slow white afternoons,
Whose eyes I knew down to their blackest depths
(Stirred by the small red smile and the white laugh)
Are married now. Some man whom I have not seen
Calls up the smile and the laugh, holds in his hands
The welcoming body, sees in the darkening eyes

Sufficient future in a smug white room.
I wish you well. May you have many sons
With darkening eyes and quiet gentle hands
To build a better future for their sons.
I, wed to history, pray for your peace:
That the smile be never twisted in your mouth,
And the pond of your mind never be rippled with sorrow:
That you may sleep your sleep as the world quakes,
And never see the chasms at your feet.

MIHAILOVICH

They kill me for the death within them. I
Follow out the pattern into night.
The last allegiance is to death. I die.
I and my works were caught in the gale of the world.

The loud mouths shall be silenced. Why should I
Outshout them now when silence answers them.
The last allegiance is to death. I die.
I and my works were caught in the gale of the world.

The final victory is in silence. I,
Inarticulate with violent men,
Learn the lilt of silence as I die.
I and my works were caught in the gale of the world.

VIRGIN COUNTRY

She has that quality of innocence,
The gravity above the laughing mouth,
The mind unburgled by experience,
Whose north is unpartitioned from its south.
Curbing that orangeman, the intellect,
Who kills the body to preserve the part,
She never fails to watch for and suspect

The mad republic shouting in the heart:
And will not die between the heart and head,
Each hunger-striking for its daily bread.

ADDRESS TO AN ABSOLUTE

Absolute, pity the visionless,
Who, knowing less than themselves, confront end walls,
Corners of rust and dust, the heart's refuse:
For pity grows flowers in the sand. At intervals,

Assuming the flesh of men, caress the pale
Uncomprehending faces deep in night,
Oceaned over by trees, star-guidance rare,
The coldness of the moon denying light.

And pity those who know more than themselves
But fail to find you, going up hills,
Naked as prayer, seeking to push a bridge
Into another time: on whom truth spills

As water-anguish in the sun-starched throat.
And, most especially, pause to pity those
Who, strangers in their time, have found no time
To stiffen their blown petals to a rose:

Standing at windows, vague as evening,
Lost in a wound, not even questioning.

THE FALLEN TREE

These fallen boughs now never more will weave
their high sky-patterns—never more receive
life from the sun. A hundred years of growing
ends here in green decay, cruel and brief.
Or is it that I, I even, remembering
the slow cadence of Autumn, swift sap-flow of Spring,
the reaching out of branch, light-search of leaf
can bring to this dead beauty some fragment of meaning?

APRIL 1940

Come through the quiet fields; April again
has brought the primroses and daily the air
grows warmer for sap flowing and leaf unfolding;
soon the green blades of corn will thrust from the bare
soil; morning be loud with bird-song
and all things eager for the coming of Spring.

There is strength here, not in the brief delight
of violet or king-cup, or the gleam
of bright wing in sunlight, but in the changing
of flower to fruit; in promise of good grain,
in the slow working of water upon stone
the quick whip of the wind, and the sting of rain.

BALLYKINLAR: MAY 1940

One standing on the empty beach
beyond the sandhills, threw wide his arms
with an oratorical gesture to beseech
the blue and unresponsive hills:

145

let now Cuchulain or some of the old gods
descend from the mountains, with chariot wheels
scything the hordes of evil, wielding again
the battle-axe for justice, before all else fails.

And yet, the Red Branch withered at the last
now only a shadow in the mind of man
the victors and the victims—they are all lost
and the shed blood forgotten.
                              Not out of the hills
must come the conquering host, but from the deep
recesses of the heart before the darkness falls.

THE MONKS AT ARDS

These have forsaken other lives and ways
And come to the north shore, to this quiet place
The sea on three sides, and to the south the trees:

Here through the silent days to pray for grace
Whether the sun shines warm or the rain falls
While the bell sounds for Vespers or Matins or Angelus

Here to shut in the heart among grey walls
Measuring all things only good or evil
By the old rigid rule that never fails.

Have you not seen the mountain-shadows at night-fall
O man with the quiet voice and the unquiet mind
Have you not heard the waves break and the gulls call?

The quiet that you seek is only found
Where heart beats not and hands are still.

THOUGHTS FROM ABROAD

In October at midnight in the olive groves
the air was warm, and the shadows lay black across
the dry earth in the moonlight, and the waves
broke in a whisper along the white sand.

In those days was the sea quite at Murlough
in the grey evening, or did rough wind lift the spray
into the larch wood, and fling the long cry
of the curlew far over bogland and ploughland?

The vines are stripped, and the oranges piled in the market,
gold in the winter sun. Snow covers the hills
taking the breath with beauty at morning and sunset.
Have the brown leaves fallen in the beechwood yet
at Mullaghmore, above the salmon falls?

Happiness runs through the fingers like water,
and was always some former time and in another country.
But now I know it was last in Glen Aray,
wild roses on the hedge, and new-cut hay by the river,
and smoke rising quietly to the evening sky.

SIERRAN VIGIL

Where the lazy wall is down
Where the lemon leaf is poisoned
Where the road is holed: where gloom of
Cloud and sky is blessing: we

Speaking no good word for war
For heroics, for the kingly dust,
Exalting not the self-evident murder,
Turn: not assuming hope: turn, offering hands.

Where blue is war zone's leading light
Where blue lights plead for morning: where
Doorways wince the darkness out:
We there, ill-starred too, offer hands.

Guitarists who with *Yi Yi Yi*
Haunted melody with reflection
Heed now the rifles' acid action
And find through fingering a new notation.

The boy with the goats takes over, takes power.
The boy with the goats, green Gabriel still,
Dyes the terraced hillsides with his Never . . .
And in his river

Here where the lazy wall is down
Here where the lemon leaf is poisoned
Where the road is holed, is trustless,
We, remembering love, kill cruelly . . .

Kill cruelty. *Hi* and you nestle in gunfire, poet!
Hi and you mow down forests briefly.
Hi and you gain the cunning touch
That low on Andalusian evenings strikes your match.

149

For this is the act, the chorus argument.
This is the work we have said is to do.
This is the thing now trust and fear both fail
We have resorted to:

Though no man here is hero, and we
Line up defending the unheroic unalterably.
Who taught us War? This time
Those who did not begin will finish it . . .

For Chico's sake, for Chica's pride . . .

And where the lazy wall is down
Where the lemon leaf is poisoned
Where the road is holed, is trustless,
Here shall we grow the olive, and the orange blithely.

THE HILLS OF POMEROY

I tried but I could not remember my dream.
I lay awake trying to recall, trying to remember it.
Did I dream that I walked on a beach
Where a boat in a swan's shape was shored, and girls
Invited to voyages with wine in goblets of gold?
Did they move softly displacing no pebbles?

I remembered I slept but it was not me sleeping:
I was not there: I was in another place . . .
While Time flickered round me like leaves,
And dolphins cruised as a fleet of starlings . . .
Was this my dream? Did I run a long way off,
Did I seek one I knew among the cedar groves
With a bow and an arrow dipped in honey?

Did she say: Are you happy? And it was you . . .
Did we gallop together through streets of wheat,
And on the immense blue tongue of the beach
Bathed without heed in a sea of silk?

I tried but I could not remember my dream.
I lay awake trying to recall, trying to remember it
By the night, by the silence, by the star at our window,
By the quiet sound of your breath, by your hair on the pillow,
By all waking things, by that one waking moment
Full of meaning and shining, the kingdom to which I awoke.

IN A VALLEY OF THIS RESTLESS MIND

I think now of latitudes solitary, Asian, and velvet,
Even while the mechanized ants march to their jungle attack,
Moving to that complete south where birds of paradise flee
In their scarlet and gold to the mating shelter of palms.

And as if wandering beneath the giant skies of the Cross,
Dissolved in the immeasurable vault that everywhere penetrates
    the Ocean,
I am borne onward through the undark where like snowflake
    silently
The white body of albatross or seaplane glides down to the swell.

Even more I am haunted by world-girdling cables
Encrusted by coral and shells, along which flash messages;
Even more I am haunted by those cables tapped by deep-sea
    creatures,
Girdling far down on the tideless sands, girdling and gripping.

Above this the mechanized ants march and birds of paradise flee
In their scarlet and gold to the mating shelter of palms.
Above this again, tier upon architectural tier of a dusking vault
Lit by a lonely wing, gliding small as snowflake and as silently.

DUBLIN BAY

Not now expecting to live forever
I can hardly remember why death seemed such fear:
Can hardly remember death is at all.

Out in the bay a coaster rides at anchor,
And faintly the hawser rattles with a dying sound—
But there has to be dying always.
Nevertheless dying is not pain:
Pain is stars through the pines and your face dark,
Your face clenched. Pain is twin lakes and a long road.
Death is the oar upright in the sands stretching away.
Death is not soon but is here as life is here.
The waves laugh, like corn sway slenderly and beckon.

VANESSA VANESSA

Three roads were shadowy and the sky over.
One road was mine with many people marching far.
One road so solitary it seemed untrodden, a road alone.
The third was rutted, old with Time and tracks, the parent road.
And at the fork of the roads Two stood: one waiting,
The other looking and wondering, anxious how she might choose.

But the waiting one, this was I, knew
There was no choice to make, or if there were
It was already too late, for her mould was setting.
And it was in that shadowy land as if my hands reached out
Not once but twice, pleadingly: once with, ah, such desire
To bring her along my road: once with sterner zeal
To set her on that lone, that solitary second path.

Twice: but each time my hands went through and fell
As if through greylit nothing: where her breasts were, arms were,
All was as shadows, though from the waist down something shrank
     in fear.
And slowly along the third, the parent road she went,
Shade fading within the shadows, lost to me, to herself,
To the world: lost and looking back.

DEIRDRE AND THE POETS

Though they have loved me as the gentle roebuck
That feeds from my hand as the dew falls on the grass,
Though they have loved me as a man might love a woman
That wanted nothing but to lift the shadows from her face,
There's been too much wagging of stale tongues these past years
And tired I am of queening shadows, sorrow's queen;
There's never one of all the lot I'd pardon,
Said the sore-tried woman of the roads.

Though they leap for the lights of the great continents
And cry from afar like the lapwing guarding his nest,
Though they talk to the wall in their towns and villages
And strive to clothe my bones in the ivy of the arch;
Yet their voices are not heard among the halls of the nations—
It's time I got me a new set of poets;
There's never one of all the lot I'd pardon,
Said the sore-tried woman of the roads.

There's never one of all the lot I'd pardon,
Unless it's all at home or far that never wrote a line
But danced and sang and dug their own or in a foreign garden,
And made their bit of money and to keep my cabin warm.
Tis them I'll choose and I will give them voices,
And no more I'll be the queen of shadows, sorrow's queen,
When their choirs like birds shall be my only poets
Said the sore-tried woman of the roads.

DIAMOND CUT DIAMOND

Two cats
One up a tree
One under the tree
The cat up a tree is he
The cat under the tree is she
The tree is witch elm, just incidentally.
He takes no notice of she, she takes no notice of he.
He stares at the woolly clouds passing, she stares at the tree.
There's been a lot written about cats, by Old Possum, Yeats, and Company,
But not Alfred de Musset or Lord Tennyson or Poe or anybody
Wrote about one cat under, and one cat up, a tree.
God knows why this should be left for me
Except I like cats as cats be
Especially one cat up
And one cat under
A witch elm
Tree.

INTERNATIONAL BRIGADE DEAD

A lonely student in a silent room
Quits his lagging pen to dream
Of thundering mountains;
Crouches, tight-faced, where the vine-stump
Spreads its silent singing leaves,
Still eyes where the lifting dust
Speaks of death;
Leaps from vine to covering vine
To the mound of safety;
Dies, as fancy has it,
Gladly on the sun's bright theatre.

An old man lifts his misty eye
To the brown ceiling of his life,
Regrets the nearness of his papered walls,
Wonders why he dared not dare
The sun to cast his leaning shadow
Forward on a page of time
Unticked by clocks on tidy mantels

A poet takes the sudden bayonet gleam to paper,
Waking hurried echoes in the huddled hills,
Not for any prideful lust or wing-clipped cause—
But for their beauty, those children of the wonder-moment,
Who dared to die in youth that youth might live.

Where the rising sun is,
Where the setting sun is,
Where the wind is
And the rain,
Where the striding spirit is
They go in their battalions,
Eager as the elements they conquered.

155

With you, O youth forever,
They shall never rest in peace.

TERROR

I lay and speculated on the impact of a bullet;
Had sight of a body spurting blood,
Sprawled helpless dying;
Clearly I saw myself erect and then
Staggered in the shock of bullets.
I saw the cold eye of the gunner,
I saw the black rim of the gun's muzzle;
I said, chewing breadcrumbs:
"In a few moments I may be dead."
Terror is kept under a steel spring;
It is the octopus in every soldier's eye
In still deep waters calm, O calm.

ALWAYS BATTLING

There is an exquisite torture in living with dull people;
Look with eyes of hate and fear
At a fine man or woman:
And the brutality of not caring,
Not feeling, not seeing, not hearing—
Not realizing at all
Things that cry aloud for vengeance.

Exterminate!
O, to have the power to exterminate
All the cruel, stupid things about.

Do you wonder that people kill themselves?
Do you wonder that people run amok and kill others?

A DUBLIN WORKER

Do you wonder that men and women fling their bodies across the
    livid mouths of guns?
Mad with fury . . .

Weep not over the shot body of a young Communist
Lying face down in the gutter.
Had you known the wild delirium of his spirit,
The accumulated hate and bitterness compressed into his brain
Until he was mad with sanity—
Had you known the fever in him,
You would laugh at the poor torn body;
The least harm they could do him—
They had done their worst before.

One and one and one and still they come,
Men and women in revolt;
Out of one dead body leaps another living.
They killed one that I might be born,
Another that you might be born.
So on and on,
Until one day they'll smother in their own creations
With all they held and had,
Leaving nothing but a book of curious stories
For some small child to criticize with smiling eyes:
"I don't believe that *all* of it is true!"

SCENE-SHIFTER DEATH

As it is true that I, like all, must die,
I crave that death may take me unawares
At the very end of some transcendent day;
May creep upon me when I least suspect,
And, with slick fingers light as feather tips,
Unfasten every little tenuous bolt
That held me all my years to this illusion
Of flesh and blood and air and land and sea.

I'd have death work meticulously too—
Splitting each moment into tenths of tenths
Replacing each infinitesimal fragment
Of old dream-stuff with new.

So subtly will the old be shed
That I'll dream on and never know I'm dead.

DEAD IN WARS AND IN REVOLUTIONS

It is cold without flesh, without bones,
To cover the soul.
No blood or nerves to take the shock, but woes
Beat on the unprotected soul.

We are naked shades within our span of life,
A gap in living fabric,
A blot, a flaw.
Cold, cold without flesh, without bones;
Cold without flesh, without bones, to cover the soul.

We can perceive the sun, but not through warmth—
We have no bodies.

159

Not through colour nor through brightness—
We've no eyes.
Not through the increase of life
Which to life it brings.
What the sun pours
On our stript souls
Is the dark inverted essence of all these things.

We know when music plays,
But we are shades;
Sounds cannot caress our ears,
And rhythm tells us only
That we have no limbs—
No muscles clean as silk to swing our joints,
No lovely ivory joints that turn and slide:
We are weightless shades,
We wait upon the wind.
Tonight the music and the wind combine
And dead things dance,
Dead leaves and dust and ghosts.

No time, no night and day—
We crave for bodily cares or even pain
To give our dreadful souls a holiday.
Our souls outcast
From kindly human insincerity
Are whitening in the savage glare of truth.

AN OLD WATERFORD WOMAN

On the road over head,
To the passers-by,
'Listen,' she said,
'Inside this cliff are the dead.
They cry
Because they are dead.'
'You hear,' said I,
'The cry
Of the wind in the hollow face
of the cliff:

Within the cliff
There is only earth.'
'And what,' she said,
'Are the dead
But earth?'

GALWAY

I know a town tormented by the sea,
And there time goes slow
That the people see it flow
And watch it drowsily,
And growing older hour by hour they say,
'Please God, to-morrow!
Then we will work and play,'
And their tall houses crumble away.
This town is eaten through with memory
Of pride and thick red Spanish wine and gold
And a great come and go;
But the sea is cold,
And the spare, black trees
Crouch in the withering breeze
That blows from the sea,
And the land stands bare and alone,
For its warmth is turned away
And its strength held in hard cold grey-blue stone;
And the people are heard to say,
Through the raving of the jealous sea,
'Please God, to-morrow!
Then we will work and play.'

PATRICK MAC DONOGH

G. M. BRADY

RHODA COGHILL

DONAGH MAC DONAGH

PATRICK MAYBIN

VALENTIN IREMONGER

BLANAID SALKELD

SEÁN JENNETT

PADRAIC FIACC

JOHN HEWITT

D. L. KELLEHER

D. J. O'SULLIVAN

ROBERT GREACEN

LESLIE DAIKEN

W. B. STANFORD

FRANCIS STUART

FREDA LAUGHTON

SAM HARRISON

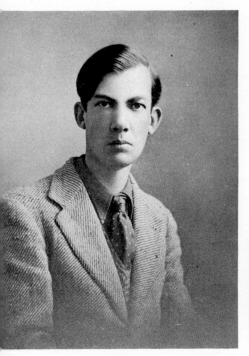

GEOFFREY TAYLOR

HARRY KERNOFF

ETHNA MAC CARTHY

ROY MC FADDEN

AUSTIN CLARKE

MARY DEVENPORT O'NEILL

DENIS WRAFTER

PADRAIC FALLON

EWART MILNE

GEORGE HETHERINGTON

PATRIC STEVENSON

BRENDA CHAMBERLAIN

EILEEN BRENNAN

THOMAS O'BRIEN

BRUCE WILLIAMSON

EILEEN SHANAHAN

D. J. O'SULLIVAN

NIGHTFALL IN INISHTRAHULL

The kittiwakes and cormorants go to sleep,
Puffins into their nesting burrows creep,
Grey-seals in their harem caverns snore,
And baby otters play beside the shore.

Click-beetles sheathe their short translucent wings,
Young bees come home with pollen laden slings,
Winged ants mate on the low sodden walls,
And garden worms come forth from tube-shaped halls.

The flowers close their petals for the night,
Daisy, violet, starwort and eyebright;
White-clover folds and crinkles as if dead,
Whilst bedstraw to the zephyrus nods its head.

An oily patch marks herring in the bay,
Beside, migrating salmon leap in play,
Elvers climb the streamlets pebbley rungs,
Where tadpoles rise to test their half-formed lungs.

Departing sunbeams linger on the tide,
Ensaffroning the wavelets far and wide,
Betwixt the clouds the moon is rising full,
Venus shines bright, night falls at Inishtrahull!

JANUARY

The scurvy-grass creeps down the strand
    Unfolding petals puce,
Red-throated divers off the land
    Replace the solan-goose,
Wild storm-toss'd seas do loudly roar,
    With white teeth chew the wrack-strewn shore.

Brown curlew congregate in flocks
   Where plashy is the clay,
Crumpled crape-lichens drape the rocks
   Bright yellow, blue and gray,
Buff throstles in the thickets hide
   From wispy winds that woosh outside.

The badger in his sett's sleep,
   And snails attached to walls;
Betimes black beetles take a peep
   From cryptic crevassed halls,
And where the hill-hare makes his seat
   Green-plover cry: "Pee-weet, pee-weet!"

MOSCHATEL

I lift my head from lowly bed
   Beside the babbling brook,
My musky smell pervades the well
   And scents the nixies' nook.

Where brown cows browse beneath branched boughs
   I drink the dew-drops bright,
My leafy sheen of glabrous green
   Glints in May's lacquering light.

No town-bred child may pick me wild
   From cracks in brick or stone,
Or city rake a poesy make
   Of my flowers for his own.

I am so small nothing at all
   Will deign to notice me,
But when stars glance and ghost-moths dance—
   I dream that I'm a tree!

LAMENT FOR SEÁN

O strong was the wood in the ashen oar,
And strong was the heart of Seán its rower,
And strong was the boat as she skimmed the tide,
And strong were the thowl-pins fixed in her side;
Strong, strong, strong!

But strong was the wave that broke the oar,
That stopped the heart of Seán its rower,
That sunk the boat as she skimmed the tide,
That smashed the thowl-pins fixed in her side;
Strong, strong, strong!

THE GLAUCOUS-GULL'S DEATH

Across the wrack besprinkled bay
The mine rode in on manes of spray,
Nigrescent, emerald, blue and white
It glittered like a stalagmite.

A glaucous-gull with wings deployed
Gyred in the gauzy azure void,
Dreamful of his late summer home
Far north on the earth's icy dome.

Within the hollows of the sea
He spied from cloudless canopy
The roundy flotsam menace shining,
Swung low with outer primaries whining.

Alit on the synthetic cover,
Indolently looked it all over,
Around the verging collar trolled
Glinting in the sun-ray's gold.

Curiously gazed at the nuts
Of the gabioned lattice-struts,
Saw the horns—salt corroded,
Pecked at one, the mine exploded!

'Rose water-spouts of many sizes,
Their funnels belching fugal noises,
Mount Etna never made more sound
Cindering the hot lavic ground.

A mighty wave ran up the shore
To tide-mark never reached before,
Withdrew again into itself,
Churning white as old Holland delf.

A smaller wave ran up again,
Three tail feathers in its long train,
Cast them now on the new tidal line,
All that was left of gull and mine.

TEMPLEOGUE

At the cross-roads I came upon the delinquent moon,
Uttering brightness even as an endless word—
Flooding all sound beside. If nestling stirred,
You could not know: all noises overstrewn
By the illimitable bright speech of the moon.
It seems, all matter into spirit blossoms
Where the hushed night birds lave their dusky bosoms
In that broad river slipping from the moon.
No other music, stir of ghost or leaf.
Look back. Over the wall, shadows of trees
Appear more dense than their realities.
Nature, run out of memory, and brief
Of thought, listens as to a tune,
Watches the slow, sweet slipping from the unlidded moon.

EVASION

The old woman has forgotten her face:
a chance mirror met, to avoid disgrace
she blinks her glance with lightning wit;
no recognition reflects in it.

The maid at the dresser drops the delph
as someone enters; she is all thumbs—
but the old woman holds on to herself,
sucking her gums.

If I didn't shrink—I am so diminished,
the old one thinks, I feel cold shy
of strange members that seem never finished
casting off and losing that thing was I.
She turns objective, for shame—in case
she might have to acknowledge her latest face.

167

MEN WALKED TO AND FRO

Spinsterish
silver
Before the shuttered window
of my dream's shelter
men walked to and fro
and wept to enter,
a while ago, ago;
but now, not so.

Not for my dance or dialect,
meaning or measure,
singing or sigh or sect;
but for youth's unelect
and common treasure.

Years, that correct, erase, perfect
faults of the spirit,
as dews, collect, collect;
left me with this defect
stamping my merit.

Mortals for no particular
are held and loved;
by what we know and are
who shall be moved?

Youth's sly departing step
echoing hollow;

love has no private lip—
begins to follow,
into oblivion's leisure,
prestissimo,
that public
gone-quick
catholic
pleasure
treasure.

LEAVE US RELIGION

Leave us religion.
We have all been given
Saints' names. Whether you call Bernadette,
Philomena, or Margaret,
And the rest—
Some pure unpressed
String echoes, under her palm,
Through an Angel's psalm,
In that still, calm,
Illumined Region—
So we are linked up with Heaven.

Man, less significant
Than the ant
With its plan of campaign—
Thinks to sting Heaven with his pain.
'Pity!' we cry, and think to rive and raid
Its golden forests with our pestilent storms:
Adulteries and deceits, the shifting forms
Of fear and hope—our follies, legion.
Yet we are starred from baptism . . . though the taints
Of infidelities divert us,
Patrons shall convert us.
We are all called after the saints;
We shall find, having left the years,
That untouched of tiredness, tears,
And flesh, Region.

A spoiled child's insurrection—
Kept from the wild flutes of our lips' election,
Dumbed like a brute,
We would refute
Authority, and bite the mother's hands.
However, she understands.
Ignorant above day's indecision
And night's derision—

Leave us religion.
Trivial flower lifts sunward chin.
Higher than tree-tip, over dust and din.
The stony finger gold-thorned for sun-polish—
If hordes demolish,
Rebuild more loftily what signals higher
Than poplar spire,
To sun-superior, light-surviving Region.
Leave us religion.
An escape? Why not. The Church is gay.
Escape, from pleasure—to nurse lepers.
The face shines plain:
Can you explain?
Successful seekers have found pleasure out;
And the escape from love, of lechers
Is a lame rout;
Dead their gaze, no inner ray.
The warring proud borne off in stretchers;
All fugitives, we should be wary steppers.

Through leafless trees, this dreary day,
Blooms at the monastery steps,
Blue and unfading, the Virgin's dress—
In every weather, clear and gay.
For no new-fangledness
Will I turn away.

We have drunk fire and eaten dirt,
Given candid beauty much hurt;
Scrawled blasphemies on city walls;
Drawn coarse jests out with bitter drawls;
Our charity was curt.

In naked celerity, remorse
Plunges out of its course,
Like a white frightened horse;
Our sins are legion.
Leave us religion.

NOW IS FAREWELL

Old man of the sea, briny bell,
I made my joy of you awhile;
But, empty mollusc, bearded shell,
Dim, under-wave, salt-crusted smile,
Now is farewell.

You are not, nor were ever mine,
Still, my unlucky star makes bald
A wilderness where you incline,
Remorse prescribing your heartscald
No anodyne.

Witless pretence learned well to wrestle.
What stealthy pleasures were compounded:
Soft flesh beneath my burning pestle—
Gold moss hair—even your blue unbounded
Gaze of a vestal.

I'd have it told to tune of harps—
That with your image I made free;
But die—to learn my will usurps.
You lift those eyes that praise the sea,
Freezing my corpse.

TERENURE

I laughed at the lovers I passed
Two and two in the shadows,—
I, solitary as one old horse I saw
Alone in the meadows.
The lovers so many I passed,
In mute embraces:
A roadside flower, joy,
In the hid places.

I wondered, sure, to notice joy
As common as a weed—
Out of my loneliness wondering,
Laughing, indeed.
I loved all the lovers I passed
Two and two, in the shadows:
I, solitary as one old horse, was standing
Alone in the meadows.

OPTIMISM

So this is life, the ranger said:
A bald brush for a bald head.
I'd get more comfort with the dead.
Man builds a house, fills a shop,
Rears gentle flower, gallant crop—
To smash up with his thunder-clap.
Self, self, eat her whelp;
Left its fur upon the shelf;
Sits alone, dumb as stone;
All she loved is dead as delph.
Spinning plane and nursery top
Hum a rhythm will not stop.
When will the adult world grow up?
We are too late too long commencing
For flights to be delight-dispensing,
Man to take down his barbed wire fencing,
And make no mischief with his breath—
In stratosphere, on lake or heath,
Whistling his gala tunes of faith
Into the empty ear of death.
I diced my way from coast to coast,
Though every rattled throw I lost.
My luck will turn when I'm a ghost.

THE DESOLATE LOVER

When I have forgotten your lips
(As I pray to God I may do),
And your voice is lost to my ears
And all the sweet that was you
Has burnt from my heart at last
Will you, too, be dead, or shall I
Be desolate dust when the thirst
And colour of living are past?

For I think while you walked with him
On the soft grass over my head
The pain that had died with my heart
Would sting in the rot of the dead.
And the old men mumble and laugh
With the love blood cold in their veins,
But I am a fire and a fear
And the house of a thousand pains,

And I walk on my burning dreams
And the hands that I touch are knives,
And breathing is death with hell
And life is a thousand lives.
And I shutter the windows now
For fear I should see the stars
And I dread that the hateful sweet
Of the moon may come through the bars.

I could take the earth in my hand
And crumple it like a flower,
I could tear the trees from their roots
In the bitterness of my power.
They say that this time is Spring
But I cannot see its glow—

God! darken the evenings down
And cover the world with snow.

Yet I know that when souls and stars
Shall meet, I may have no rest—
I shall see them walk hand in hand,
Her head on his hated breast.

SHANKILL

The happy road that brought me here
   Runs on alone to Bray
Why need I follow it so far
   And waste this golden day
   Upon the white highway?

Wild currant grows along the hedge,
   The wind is sharp and sweet,
And I can hear the brisk sea run
   On white exultant feet
   Where field and shingle meet.

The stream I follow in its race
   I cannot tell its name
I only know the brown trees bend
   Their leafless heads for shame
   And April is to blame.

And here where water music plays
   There is no you nor I
Nor town nor tears nor heaviness
   But only wide blue sky—
   Perhaps a butterfly.

THE KILKENNY BOY

He sang an old song
And the hawthorn pushed
Through the lines of fence
That were the words.

The wet hawthorn budded
All through his song
And a lonely lilt
Came into his voice.

His eyes were shallow
And young as Pan's,
His dappled eyes
Of fern and heather.

(I saw the dark hills
And the fairy boy
Leaping the streams
With his goatskin flying)

He sang an old song
And his voice was sweet
With the undropped tears
Of men at Cove.

He sang of Eire
But his eyes were wild
Of the days when she
Was too young for a name.

EPIPHANY

A small house with a pointed roof
A window kind with light
And overhead one watchful star
And all about the night.

A weary man who waits on God
A woman worn with tears—
On such as these the star has shone
Serenely through the years.

The cradle of a little child
The lamplight on the floor—
Three shadow Kings with shadow gifts
Come silent to the door.

The man, the woman and the babe,
Toil, sacrifice and pain—
The Kings kneel to the trinity
And Christ is come again.

ANGELUS-TIME NEAR DUBLIN

At twelve bell answers bell.
The city's notes
are sudden and grave with archangelic throats.
One later bell,
over the tranquillizing air delayed,
down from the hill's hedge-quilted fields and seaward-tilted lanes,
has a lilied voice, slender, virginal unafraid.

At twelve bell answers bell,
as Mary to Gabriel.

TO A GREEK SHIP IN THE PORT OF DUBLIN

The *Cleanthes* of Andros
with a blue-striped flag and a crew of swarthy faces
was anchored down at City Quay
freighted with olive oil and vinous raisins.

Two sailors caught the accent of my words
when I spoke a welcome in half-remembered phrases.
Tall, honey-skinned, sun-glancing men they were.
Very easily they might have mocked.
I trusted in some antique courtesy.
They did not laugh. So we were ancient friends.

For once, very long ago, the sons of an Irish king
sailed eastwards to visit Tuis, King of Greeks,
for the sake of a magical all-healing pigskin.
And other princes of the Gaelic speech
encountered golden heroes from Byzantium.
And from the exploits of each
the scathing singers of Eire and the suaver singers of the Greeks

distilled the most radiant sagas of the Western World and East,
from the Euxine to our Ocean of the Hesperides,
from our Moy Mel to the Colchian plain of Medea's sorceries.

Such was the equality of our nations' lineage—
from epic heroes and from lavish kings—
and we, drinking barley-brew in a quayside pub,
were glad and sad, remembering splendours of past things;
when the *Cleanthes* of Andros
with blue-striped flag and a crew of swarthy faces
was anchored down by the slums at City Quay
freighted with glistening olive oil and raisins.

This, three years past. No visit now from those Greek ships,
and in Greece now no sweetness of grape, no oil to brighten dry
    lips,
no laughter, no dancing, no welcome for the eager pilgrim-guest
to those ancient stones that of all carved shapes are shaped loveliest,
over whose unhungering marble there is no conquest.

BEFORE SALAMIS

The Persian galleys plumed with warriors
move, dolphin-curved, across the ivory sea.
Flutes set a speed for oars. King Xerxes broods
above the bay and prays to barbaric gods.

Greece stirred at dawn. At sunrise raised shields gleamed
and trumpet-calls set all the caves and cliffs
ablaze with sound.
                            And up Cithaeron's roads
in lonely farmsteads mothers caught the cry—
faint as a serpent's hiss, and horrible—
and clasped their children in the shadowy rooms.

UNDERTONE

When the landfolk of Galway converse with a stranger,
softly the men speak, more softly the women,
light words on their lips, and an accent that sings
in traditional cadences (once plucked by harpists
to cheer melancholic carousals of kings),
when the landfolk of Galway converse with a stranger.

But under the cadences, under the light lips,
under the lilt of the harp-plucking bard,
threaded deep in its socket of anger and loneliness
a passion, with piercing and tightening screw, grips
their minds' inner engine and presses it hard.

When the landfolk of Galway converse with a stranger,
softly the men speak, more softly the women;
yet older than harp-playing, older than welcomes,
an undertone threatens Fomorian danger,
when the landfolk of Galway converse with a stranger.

CORN CAÑON

Wet, wayward fingers of the west wind wave the wheat,
Bow the barley, chafe the corn in swinging rhythmic sequences
  complete.
Long, serried ranks of cereals, kowtowing, bowing
        Shaking, quaking,
                Shivering, quivering,
Shedding grain grace notes (drops from every joint)
In liquid figuration of unheard counterpoint.

Such is the visual, patterned music that I watch
Whose polyphonic sound is lost. I catch
Only the wind's melodic line, whining, pining,
        Sighing, crying,
                Swishing, wishing
To lisp its secrets to a million reeds
Or tongue its trouble through a waste of weeds.

DOGROSE

White, stamen-shadowed petals of wild rose
Now hold their shallow chalice in the hedge,
Through folded buds, which calyxes enclose,
Drives nature's gentle, but all-splitting wedge;
And I am led to think of seas—not these
Trim, inland fields—of dizzy, cliff-top edge
        Where, lost to bees,
A rose braves every wind that blows—not those
Mid-county flowers in bee-besieged hedgerows.

For so contrasting elements impress,
Encompassing extremes of bold and meek.
What did the fragile flower's pale loveliness

181

Not gain by blooming in a place so bleak?
And what earth-quaking shocks did not the rocks
Receive from five frail petals, wan and weak?
        Brute force may box
And seem to win; but in each rose there grows
A greater power and mastery than blows.

AUTUMNAL CONSUMMATION

The year grows darker, but each day more lamps
Of leaves illumine hedge and forest till
The chestnuts' incandescence passes amps
More power than when they blew the fuse of spring,
And I roam through gold woodlands wondering,
Or gaze on beauty from my creepered sill.

More lamps light daily as the year grows old.
Who knew dull, August green-ness held such wealth?
It is as if the hoarded, hidden gold
Of many misers suddenly was poured
From out the clammy vaults where it was stored
Clandestinely by stratagem and stealth.

And, all around, the brush-wood is arrayed
(Each may twig now with clotted blood drops bleeds)
In berry brooch and necklace lately made
From polished hip and haw; and, see, where flies
Sought bindweed flower through holly bush, there lies
Upon its head of thorns a crown of beads.

ANGLO-EIRE VIGNETTE

Parting friends put me the query,
'Do you call that country "Eerie"?
Or', continued their enquiry,
'Maybe it is spoken "Ireie",

HARRY KERNOFF R.H.A.

"A BIRD NEVER FLEW ON ONE WING"

"Aerie", "Error", "Era", "Ire"?
Or does one pronounce it "Air"?'
And I answered in despair—

'If it is your real desire
To pronounce correctly, share a
Secret, think of "De Valaira"
And you have the spoken "Eire".'
'But *we* call him "De Valèera"—
Is that also a chimera?'
'Well, 'though 'tis the "devil's era"

There it is the devil's Eire.'
'But . . . "De Vàlera"—is that
Wrong as well?' I raise my hat
Shouting as their engines rev.
'Call *an Taoiseach* simply "Dev."
And that most distressful dire land
He'd rechristen, merely . . . "Ireland".'

SOUTHERN SUMMER

Now are the forests dark and the ways full
Of foliage and grass and heavy branch,
And the green darkness stirs like a deep pool.
Beneath the groping foot unseen things crunch
While flat hot leaves slip past the upturned face,
And the warm-scented vapour after rain
Hangs in the gloom, and nowhere in that place
Is thinnest bird-note. All the heavy pain
Of earth is on me. Now are the forests dark—
And you lie sleeping in some far-off room.
Oh would that I could see you stand up stark
And pale and fountain-like against the gloom
Of over-burdened things, you slim and cool.
Now are the forests dark and the ways full.

UNE IDOLE DU NORD

She dwells, pale midnight sun, beyond the river
Yellow and sullen beneath the northern wind;
And north the dark sky closes in, for never
Has trail led north of this, nor mind
Sent thoughts more north, nor followed
Where never even bird has lit the tide
White with its breast. Nor ever has white fox
Slunk north through forest snow as far as this,
Where mountainous white shells uprear fire-hollowed
Crests, and down the darkness white fields slide,
While ice-choked caverns echo volcanic murmur,
And midnight lights glint on the frozen rocks;
Into dead air steam columns, boiling, hiss
And fall in hail. O God, the only summer
Is on her lips, and even they have lied.

COOGAN'S WOOD

They played till the dusk of summer in the wood
By the stream full of boulders under the hill;
And now like a shadow and bell within my blood
Their cries and the wood in the dusk are throbbing still.

Fold me once more, dark leaves, shelter the earth
And men from the desert heat and fevered din
Of war. Sweetness blooms there and there sways mirth
And deep in the stream-lit dusk peace blossoms within.

Ah, children do you go there summer days
Or are you too old now still to race and cry
From pool to pool? And is it only I
Who turn once more along those dusky ways
Into that wood, into that world, from one
Where life is shrunk to what can be fired from a gun?

THE UPPER LAKE

Be dark, be deep, wait there for me between
The hills, wild lake, I will return once more;
One evening, late and weary will I lean
Against a boulder by your darkening shore
Under the fir-trees. There, there will I come
When I am tempered, deepened, stilled as you.
Then will the time be ripe and I ripe too
At last to stand beside you and be dumb.

IRELAND

Over you falls the sea-light, festive yet pale,
As though from the trees hung candles alight in a gale
To fill with shadows your days, as the distant beat
Of waves fills the lonely width of many a Western street

Bare and grey and yet hung with berries of mountain ash,
Drifting through ages, with tilted fields awash,
Steeped with your few lost lights in the long Atlantic dark,
Sea-birds' shelter, our shelter and ark.

Berlin 1944

BOAT-HAVEN, CO. MAYO

That house, a stone's throw from the shell-strewn shore,
Now nearly swallowed by encroaching trees
That creep upon it from the hill behind,
Itself a shell like any of these, gaping
And broken but still beautiful, was built
By Smuggler Jordan in seventeen-twenty or so.
      Gable and wings toward the crumpled sea,
With vacant door and window, yet look out
Through unkempt hair of overgrowth—the door
And lower windows all but blocked by nettles—
In the spare sunlight and tart air of autumn.
What once were lawns remain like lawn, kept clipt
By sandhill-warrened rabbits, to high tide;
While of the garden, one exotic fig-tree
Still struggles strangled by black-fruited brambles.
      Then who on earth was Jordan? I don't know.
Only his name survives among the peasantry.
English perhaps, a bit rough-tongued no doubt;
He may have had a palate for French wine
Or brandy landed on this awkward coast
Too intricate for revenue men to watch;
But he had certainly an eye for building,
Or else employed an architect who had.
      So, granted an eye for a right elevation,
A nice taste, too, in moulding and stuccoed brick,
Let me suppose he judged a face and figure,
Manner and heart, with justice; had in fact
A wife who'd grace the landscape and the house;
Who'd read Matt Prior and not forget her prayers;
Cold-curved, demure, and coyly courteous
At picnics or when company would dine;
Coiled and familiar in her feather bed;
High-breasted and bright-eyed—a girl for whom
It might have been delight, with contraband

Of coarser kind, to land French silks and ribands.
      One idly speculates, because one must
People a place—if only to complete
The picture for a sentiment.

                            However,
Now all that's left after two hundred years—
A name and this facade that keeps a name
Still faintly in men's memory—will go;
For there's enough cut stone in coping and lintel
Still to call forth a natural cupidity
In any native who's a byre to build.

FROM AN IRISH-LATIN MACARONIC

O dark-haired girl, let us now
    Forget this stark philosophy
That's cracked and cold as blackthorn bough
    Wind-broken on the tree.
        Though it be honourable and high,
        Bitter it is and crooked and dry.

Let us unrobe mind from such thought
    As our bodies cast off old clothes,
Borrowed or bartered or bought—
    King's gift or so-and-so's;
        And let who will take it,
        If we need new we'll make it.

A slave under slave-whip sting
    Cried 'Mortify the flesh',
An emperor, whose mind's wing
    Was caught in belly's mesh,
        Turned all thought to sour sadness
        Because of belly's badness.

But let us, neither slave nor sick,
    Take joyfully what gifts gods give
Nor fear their rods nor their whips' flick.

TURF-GIRL

And love; for but by love we live;
  And Love, dark head, is all the power
  That breaks the green bough into flower.

BLUEBELL

(From a picture by Renoir)

Time taken by the forelock as he flies,
  Love tamed with casual care,
Slow smile of sloe-dark eyes,
  And hyacinthine hair.

Time tied and tucked away to groom,
  Tidy in little room compressed
By grip of slow-expanding womb
  Below bloom-brindled breast.

Time to be pastured out once more
  Past parted coralline pink portal
Grown great from grace and groaning sore,
  From mortal, immortal;

Lo, Love in freckled fleet surprise
  Stares where unflickering stare
Slow-smiling sloe-dark eyes
  From hyacinthine hair.

SONG

Rousing to rein his pad's head back
  And turning his own to stare
Up along Kentish downland track
  Spider-bright in the April air,
Oh! said the Pilgrim Chaucer,
  O, copper-coin her hair.

With Wop his dog in a Warwick lane
  And never a sonnet's sigh or care
Till, lifting an eye from the ripening grain,
  And all his wits at once aware,
Oh! said the Stratford Country Squire,
  O, carrots for her hair.

'Way back early from Hampton Court,
  Less than normally here or there,
Fumbling after the right retort—
  Epigram, epitaph, into prayer—
Oh! said my Lord of Rochester,
  O, for her Titian hair.

Well, after these—and one may suppose
  Well after these and some to spare—
All with differently qualified oh's,
  A different view of a fair affair,
O who were you in a bus to say
  Oh! for her bonny red hair?

Nor, under and under not her hat
  The rarely covered or rarer bare,
By proof not flame-proof, this with that
  Who are you yet who dare compare?
Oh! coppery, carroty, Titian O,
  Her rust-red autumn-beech-leaf hair.

AFTERNOON IN ANGLO-IRELAND

A mute bird sidles through soft valleys of air
And the land is stripped to its golden skin of corn.
Like a teasing diaphragm, the hills twitch with heat
And deck-chairs creak on the lawn.
Beyond us, the Pilgrim's road, and the bare feet
Of penitents, even now bleeding into the dust, aware
Of hedges not as high as they were.

The blossoms stir, and petals drop like tears
Falling deep into your hair, darling, deep as the inclination
To remember our past. We rest on a trestle of shadow
And joke that we're dead but uncoffined. Our one expectation
Is never to be forgiven. Children shout from the meadow,
But how can we know them, whose eyes and whose ears
Never see what we see or hear what we hear?

The hedgerows grow numb with bees
But there is silence among the birds. They are quiet
And bright-eyed out of the sun. A scythe hisses
Like silk against silk. There is only a visual riot
Of summer, a stillness of frightened kisses.
There is terror alone with us here under the trees.
The yellow scrolls of sunlight fall like rejected pleas.

The end is almost with us. But never expect
The tight, jealous mercy of water, the swift lunge of fire.
Await only the end of that pilgrimage others are making,
Prayer, penitence and a sacrifice whose altar is no higher
Than where we sit. There will be no leavetaking,
For none of us stays, none will connect
Our past and our future. There are no debts to collect.

There is still time for a walk by the river,
So sinewy in winter, and in summer, white circles of foam

Drifted, we said, like drowning butterflies.
But we were children then, and looked on this as home
And this was where we brought whatever prize
We won elsewhere. Now we can only summon a shiver
Of remembrance, that our love has betrayed such a lover.

A trifle of sound crumples the smooth blue air
And shadows fall like gages on the grass.
We are most conscious of evening, of the tidal dusk
Leaving its wrack of darkness. We watch it pass,
Drawn into the horizon. The moon's long tusk
Jabs at the windows, twists across the stair. . . .
Perhaps, indeed, our beauty is bred of fear.

The blotted glass of the river breaks and re-shapes,
But there is only blackness behind blackness, an inward reflection
Of justice. The pilgrims, bent on vengeance, will return
Down our quiet road. Love, at a narrow deflection,
Flies out like a bird from the laurels. I burn
For a kiss of hope, but hope escapes
Like a pelted dog in the streets.

Will they worship us dead? Will they observe our fast day?
For us, life was a long hunger. The rarest food
Turned to ash on our tongues, the most delicate wine
Went sour in our cellars. The bad and the good
Surrendered their qualities. We weakened the structure ourselves,
    and the mine
Caved in upon us. We are so transient, so fay
It is small wonder that we went astray.

Those we lived with never came to our parties, but sometimes sang
To our guests, or sat in the servants' hall,
Moody and spiteful and quick to disown
Their contempt. Above stairs, the ball
Danced to its end, and the host stood alone
On his steps, watching the trees as they sprang
Into the rushing polka of the wind.

We never learnt to keep time to flute, fiddle or drum.
We have forgotten to play ourselves. It is doubtful, even,
If there is music left in us at all.
We must go, yet cannot leave. Hell or heaven. . . .
We get no choice, whether we rise or fall.
Fold up the deck-chairs, dear. There will be some
Not needed next year, no matter how warm the sun.

A THOUGHT FOR MY LOVE

The stars catch my eyes;
All the bright harness of heaven
Jingles in soft surmise.
The night is a team gently driven
To morning; stabled and put to ease
In the early victorious hours.

Your love is my care,
Your shadow falls on my place—
The tree over the stream, the share
Of defeat in a moment. Your face
And your mind are my cup and its draught;
Your hands are the hands of my craft.

Into the spacious granary of day
You, childlike, come.
Here all the words you say
Rejoice in the harvest-room.
Dear love, guide me now in your faith,
Quit me of stubborn death.

HOMAGE OF WAR

Across the barrage, the cities of Europe remember
The lovers that paced in their parks, that in spring
To walk was to waltz like the flowers in a border

With the soft caracole of the breeze, and they sing
To the shells and the bombers intent on their murder.

Impatient and lovely, some trees still have their leaves
In green shawls about them. The undershot jaw of the sky
Will menace their magic and rinse them
With words that are bullets and fire, with hate that's a lie
Turned in on itself, an ignoble ransom.

The young are apart and their love has become
A strained girl in the house, a man with no thought of her
That war can't suppress. And the roses he sees
Have petals that grow round a wound, a flower no wind can stir:
These cannot be dressed into bouquets. They are not for praise.

When the smoke drifts away like a drunkard,
The crazy harangue of the guns is better than silence.
Death is a better end than to be accused
By the unpeopled streets, or by the cool, tense
Shadow of courage from those whom the battle erased.

The conquered are always at fault. The white throat
Slipped under a knife, a soul that breathes through its bruises
Is only temptation, man's wicked thought in the night.
After its falcon dive, the soul gently cruises,
Lost in voluted space without compass or light.

There's no escape to the future, no rest in the present.
A terrible homage this is, on broken knees, in death's hall,
And the inward man contentedly breathing
As if admiring the murals on the execution wall,
As if grateful for his stark historic fading.

FOR M—

It is not easy to be less than lovers,
I think it is simpler far
To catch the wind's bridle,

Thrust up and ride between the cheering trees
Bank upon bank of leafy throatiness,
Fulfilling once again
What the sun had promised for us
Of partnership and pain.
Each year attends our downfall
And yet does something more
Than shift a subsoil
Grant an acre less
To this poor family.
The nursery's kingdom now stands out of doors
The golliwog reigns in terror on the hill
And shakes his startled locks against the sky.
Now is the time to thank
Our stars for their exciting twist and curl.
Though drunken in their cradles
They dare better
To settle finally for ever
What cut our veins and jerked our feet away.

Should the hawk and the oyster mate
Surprise would not halt us,
The slighting and chiding of lovers
Call no correction.
We know too well that those in partnership
Break down each other's health.
Why should we die this way,
Tense as a drill of light on the open sea,
We who had ankles and poise
And fists to crack nuts in,
We who as children understood cruelty?
Long ago in a big house they danced
And pair by pair they left me.
But the woman I could not touch
Stayed by the fire.
Oh, when at last I slept,
Who was I to know
She was the only one who kept
Her promise and her way of speaking.
This is my question: Was she the one

Who ran, her head above the cornstalks, laughing,
When she was twelve?
Who said: Is it true we must bear it,
This vast undoing of hate?
Yes, then as children
We must have teased and chattered in the sun.
The drift and catch of the wind
Came to us easily,
Came to us then.

THE OLD MAN TO HIS SCYTHE

Old scythe in the hedge,
You're a fright with the rust,
Though myself's little better,
Had I thought of it first!
And to think of the times
And the joys we have known,
When my hone and my stone
Drew a song from your steel;
Such a music we made
In the fields of Ardheel,
When the midges danced jigs
And the sun lavished gold
On the fields of Ardheel—
And the feel of your ash,
And the swish and the flash—
O, barley fell fast
In the fields of Ardheel!
Then Mary would come
With a mugful of milk
And a carraway cake—
Such a smoke I would have
Sitting there in the shade,
While my hone and my stone
Put an edge on your blade;
Sitting there in the shade,
I called you my jewel,
And my sweet little tool,
O, the music we made
In the fields of Ardheel!
And to think of you now
Lying down in your rust,
And to think of myself
That's soon to be dust.

ON HEARING A BROADCAST OF CEREMONIES IN CONNECTION WITH CONFERRING OF CARDINALS' HATS

When old heads felt to-day
The silk of scarlet hats
To Heaven were radio-cast
Lauds and magnificats,

As if such pompous praise
To Him were sweeter noise
Than that of growing grass
Or lambs or infant joys!

SABBATH REFLECTION

He strode along the chapel aisle,
Tall and lissom, free of guile,
The rain that cleansed the golden whin
Pearling on his freckled skin.

I saw a high one in her pew,
A lady—only that I knew—
Stare at him with greedy eyes,
Then curl her lips on brief apprise.

Quite handsome in his way, no doubt,
But after all—a country lout:
'Twas so I felt the harlot say
As she knelt proudly down to pray.

GEORGE M. BRADY was born in 1917, in Co. Clare, spent his early years in England and then settled in Dublin. He likes Beethoven, walking in mountainy country and talking to strangers. His favorite poets are Donne, Blake, Byron, Hopkins, Yeats and Eliot, and yet his political allegiance is to the left. He is married and has one child. Like many of his countrymen he now earns his livelihood in England. His poetry has been published in *The Bell, Irish Times, Dublin Magazine, Horizon, New Statesman and Nation, Harpers' Bazaar* and in various anthologies.

EILEEN BRENNAN was born in England in 1913, of Irish parents active in the Irish independence movement. She was educated at the Convent of the Sacred Heart, Newcastle-on-Tyne, St. Mary's Training College, Fenham, and the National College of Art, Dublin. Before marrying journalist Brian O'Neill, she was a school teacher. Her work has appeared in most Irish poetry periodicals and in several anthologies. She lives in Dublin.

AUSTIN CLARKE was born in 1896 in Dublin and received his education at University College, Dublin. At the age of 21, he published his first book of verse and gradually became one of Ireland's most prolific poets. Known chiefly as a poet's poet, his natural modesty and the obscurity of his references have tended to keep from him some of the recognition he deserves. In 1936, his collected poems were published by Macmillan, but they are no longer in print. In 1938 a slim volume of 12 lyrics, *Night and Morning* appeared in Dublin, from which all but one of the present selections were taken. "This book," says Robert Farren, "more than any of his books, is *he* himself as a person saying his say. But in it he speaks so arcanely, lurks and skulks in such pitchy corners of language that what he says is often matter for debate." In 1939 Clarke began broadcasting regularly and since then has directed his talents to writing, producing and publishing a number of verse plays for broadcasting and for the theatre. He lives in Templeogue, Co. Dublin.

BRENDA CHAMBERLAIN of Irish, Manx and English ancestry (says she feels most strongly the influence of her Irish grandmother) was born in North Wales in 1912, spent five years as an art student in London and visited abroad—otherwise has continued to live in North Wales on the island of Bardsey off the Welsh coast, where she paints, writes poetry and experiments with prose. Her paintings, including the self-portrait in this book, were exhibited in London in 1948 and got favorable mention for their "vigour and unconventionality." "I am only at home in mountains, or on the sea; I dislike crowds, regionalism and nationalism . . . distrust brain without heart," she writes.

RHODA COGHILL was born in Dublin in 1903, and was educated as a musician at the University of Dublin. She became a concert pianist and pianaforte teacher, and, in 1939, accompanist at Dublin Broadcasting Station. While recovering from a long illness she took to writing poetry as a pastime. Her poems have been appearing in Irish literary periodicals ever since. She lives in Dublin.

HUGH CONNELL was born in London in 1896. "With the exception of two years secondary education in England and a few months in eastern France," he reports, "the remaining time has been spent living and farming on the family property in Munster." His poems have appeared in the *Dublin Magazine*. He makes woodcuts as a hobby.

MAURICE JAMES CRAIG was born in Belfast in 1919. He received his education at Magdalene College, Cambridge and at the University of Dublin. He has contributed to most of the Irish and English magazines of verse and is represented in several anthologies. In 1948 he published his first serious prose, *The Volunteer Earl*, the life and times of James Caulfield.

LESLIE DAIKEN was born in Dublin in 1912. He is a graduate of Trinity College, Dublin. Has worked as factory-hand, salesman, script-writer of documentary films and radio programs. He served as a private in the "Eire Army" during the first years of World War II; later as a special correspondent for Reuters in London. He has compiled and edited two collections of modern Irish writing. In 1945 a volume of his verse, *Signatures of All Things*, was published in London.

JOHN LYLE DONAGHY was born in northern Ireland in 1902 and educated at Larne Grammar School and at Trinity. A teacher and a journalist, he has published a number of books of verse and verse-drama, all limited editions, hard to come by. He lives in County Wicklow.

PADRAIC FALLON was born in Athenry, Galway in 1906 and was educated at the Trappist Monastery in Roscrea. He is a Customs & Excise official at Wexford, which brings him into contact with sailors, fishermen, yachtsmen, farmers and other people from all over. Aside from poetry he is interested in pantheistic philosophy and folk-lore, sailing a small boat, and in starting a verse magazine. He thinks poets are underpaid. "No payment," he writes, "is quite good enough for any good poem." The Gaelic influence in his verse is strong. His work has appeared in many literary publications in Ireland and England. Many consider him Ireland's best living poet.

PADRAIC FIACC was born in Belfast in 1924. He came to America in 1930 and lived in New York for seventeen years before returning to Belfast in 1946, as a citizen of Eire. While in this country he studied for the priesthood but was unable to continue because of poor health. Padraic Colum and Michael McLaverty have influenced his thinking as well as his poetry. His work has appeared in *The Irish Times, Irish Bookman* and *Catholic World*. He has set for himself an ambitious literary career.

MONK GIBBON was born in Dublin in 1896, the son of a clergyman. Educated at St. Columba's College, Rathfarnham, and Keble College, Oxford, he served in the British Army 1916-1918, and later studied farming in Jersey. He has taught in Switzerland, England and Ireland, travelled extensively and is at present settled in Killybegs, Co. Donegal. His published work includes: *For Daws to Peck At*, 1929, *Seventeen Sonnets*, 1932, *The Seals*, 1935. He also edited and introduced the AE Memorial Volume, *The Living Torch*. His first major prose work, *Mount Ida*, was published in 1948.

ROBERT GREACEN was born in 1920 in Londonderry. He attended Queen's University, Belfast, and Trinity College, Dublin, where he learned to like D. H. Lawrence and Joyce. Has contributed poetry and criticism to *The Bell, Horizon* and other literary periodicals and published two volumes of verse. In 1946 he edited *Irish Harvest,* an excellent collection of contemporary Irish writing. In 1948 he collaborated with Valentin Iremonger in an anthology of contemporary Irish poetry somewhat similar to the present volume. In the same year he published a collection of his own poetry, *The Undying Day.* He is married and lives in Dublin.

SAM HARRISON was born in Co. Armagh in 1920 and was educated at Armagh Royal School and Trinity College, Dublin. He defines poetry as "a specialized use of words for communicating emotions and sensations with a particular personal significance", and admits to being influenced by poet W. R. Rodgers. His work has appeared in *The Bell, The Irish Times* and other periodicals, and in several anthologies. He is married and lives in Switzerland.

GEORGE HETHERINGTON was born in Dublin in 1916; educated at Baymount, Dublin and Bromsgrove, Worcestershire, England. A printer by profession, he is a director of Hely's Ltd., Dublin printers. Married and has two children. He likes to grow roses and keep bees.

JOHN HEWITT was born in Belfast in 1907, the son of a school-teacher. He is a graduate of Belfast University and is presently Keeper of the Art Division, Belfast Museum and Art Gallery. Sponsor and chief protagonist of the Ulster Regionalist Movement, he believes the future of culture lies in smaller communities, "that poetry grows out of knowledge, craftsmanship, sincerity, and love, and that its imagery should be concrete." Himself influenced by Robert Frost and Lewis Munford, Hewitt has encouraged most of the younger crop of Northern Irish writers. His poetry has appeared in many anthologies and a selection is soon to be published in London.

VALENTIN IREMONGER was born in 1918. He is in the Irish diplomatic service; has acted, studied stage production and written a great deal of poetry. In 1945 he won the AE Memorial Award of £100 given once every 5 years for "the best literary work, either creative or scholarly, by an Irish writer under 35." The prize volume of poems, *Reservations,* is soon to be published. Co-author with Greacen and Williamson of *On the Barricades,* a short anthology of poetry, he collaborated with Greacen in a much more ambitious anthology of contemporary Irish poetry soon to be published in London. He is married and lives in Dublin. Iremonger thinks it high time the Irish overseas stopped harping on the 700 years of persecution theme— "it's history, it's fact, but it's over," he reports. He likes the poetry of John Crowe Ransom, Allen Tate and other modern Americans.

SEÁN JENNETT works for a London publishing house, where he specializes in book design and typography. Faber and Faber have published two volumes of his verse, *Always Adam* (1943) and *The Cloth of Flesh* (1945). He describes himself and his poetry somewhat as follows: "I had the misfortune to be born in England when my father was in the Army and my family led a gypsy existence—as indeed it always has. I find that in England everybody listens to my speech and immediately decides that I must be Irish; when I am in Ireland I am taken for an Englishman. It is not until I get into the Gaeltacht and can talk in Irish that the mantle of green descends upon me. I find myself omitted from anthologies of English poets on the ground that I am an Irishman and from anthologies of Irish poets on the ground that I have grown English. I do feel myself an Irishman, as I ought with so many O's and Macs in my ancestry and it is hard to be omitted from Irish collections—more so if it is realized that the structure of my verse owes more to Gaelic verse than perhaps that of any other Irish poet."

DANIEL LAWRENCE KELLEHER was born in Cork. He was educated by the Christian Brothers and in 1905 was graduated from University College, Cork. He has taught school in England, written a dozen travel books and five volumes of verse. His play, *Stephen Gray,* was put on at the Abbey Theatre. He is married and lives in Dublin. He likes to tell of being taken to visit the poet Canon P. A. Sheehan at Doneraile in 1911. " 'What is your ambition?' said the Canon to me. 'I would like to write during my time five poems that would be remembered after me,' said I. The Canon hesitated, looked at me and then said meditatively, 'that is a lot.' "

HARRY KERNOFF was born in London in 1900. At the age of fourteen he moved with his family to Dublin, where he studied at the Metropolitan School of Art. In 1923 he won a scholarship and continued his art studies in London, Paris, and in the U.S.S.R. He has had 15 one-man exhibitions in addition to illustrating a number of books. Two collections of his woodcuts have been published in book form. Interested in all forms of artistic expression, he was elected to the Royal Hibernian Academy in 1935.

FREDA LAUGHTON was born in Bristol in 1907. She studied art in London for four years and later taught it. In 1932 she moved to Ireland where she has lived ever since—presently on a farm in Co. Down. Married to an Irishman, her favorite hobby is writing and illustrating delightful tales of phantasy for their daughter. She began writing poetry in 1942 and her first book of poems, *A Transitory House* was published in 1945; a second is on the way.

ETHNA MacCARTHY was born in the North of Ireland and has lived most of her life in Dublin. She is a grand-daughter of Denis Florence MacCarthy, young Ireland poet of the 1850's. A practising physician and at the same time a lecturer in Spanish and French at Trinity College, Dublin, she manages to find time to write prose as well as poetry. Her translations of medieval Spanish ballads have appeared in the *Dublin Magazine* and elsewhere, and her poems have been published in the *Irish Times* and in several anthologies.

DONAGH MacDONAGH was born in Dublin on St. Cecilia's Day, 1912, the son of Thomas MacDonagh, 1916 poet and revolutionary leader. He was educated at University College, Dublin, where he edited the college magazine, and in France. He was called to the bar in 1936. He has published verse and prose in Irish, English and American magazines and currently broadcasts in Dublin. Interested in folklore, ballads and Dublin dialect, which he collects. He is married, has two children and lives in Dublin. A book of verse, *Veterans,* was followed in 1946 by a verse play, *Happy as Larry* which has achieved considerable success on the stage. In 1947 a second volume of poetry, *The Hungry Grass* appeared.

PATRICK MacDONOGH was born in 1902. He was educated at Avoca School and Trinity College, Dublin, where he was more interested in athletics than the arts. Taught for a couple of years and did commercial black-and-white work. He contributed verse to the *Irish Statesman, The Observer* and other papers in the 1920's but published nothing between 1929 and 1941, since when he has appeared frequently in *The Dublin Magazine* and other Irish literary periodicals. Has published four books of verse and been included in many anthologies. In America his poetry has appeared in *Harpers, '47, The American Mercury, Tomorrow,* and the *Kenyon Review.*

ROY McFADDEN was born in Belfast in 1921 during the 'Trouble.' He lived in that city until 1941 when a bomb sent him to Downpatrick, and then to Lisburn where he now lives. Is a solicitor by profession. He has published three books of poetry, *Swords And Ploughshares* (1943), *Flowers For A Lady* (1945), and *The Heart's Townland* (1947). Two novels remain unpublished. He respects Yeats, admires AE and owes allegiance to Blake.

PATRICK MAYBIN was born in 1916 in Lisburn, Co. Antrim, the son of a schoolmaster. A graduate of Medical Faculty, Belfast University, he served with distinction in the Royal Army Medical Corps in North Africa and Italy during World War II. His verse and his prose reportage have appeared in Irish journals and in anthologies.

EWART MILNE was born in 1903 in Dublin where he received his education. Has been a school-teacher, a sailor before the mast and a Medical Aid volunteer on the Loyalist side during the Spanish war. He has published five books of verse. He is married and now lives in Essex, England.

THOMAS O'BRIEN was born in Dublin in 1914 "of working class stock." He left school at fourteen and started contributing short stories to religious periodicals. At nineteen he joined Sinn Fein and the I.R.A., and later the Communist Party. Fought in Spain with the International Brigade. Now lives in Bray, County Wicklow, where he supports a family by writing detective stories and westerns.

MARY DEVENPORT O'NEILL was born in Galway and was educated at Eccles Street College and the National College of Art, Dublin. She is married to Joseph O'Neill, administrator and novelist, and lives in Dublin. Her chief interest is in combining ballet with acting and verse-speaking in the performance of verse plays. *Bluebeard* was produced in 1933 and *Cain* in 1945. In 1929 Cape published *Prometheus and Other Poems.*

DANIEL JAMES O'SULLIVAN is a lighthouse keeper on the coast of Donegal. He was born in Whitegate, Co. Cork, in 1906 of a family of lighthouse keepers. He left school at the age of 12 and took various jobs. He is a keen field naturalist who has done valuable work on the plants and animals of the island of Inistrahull, adding several new species to the list of Irish flora and fauna. Of his poetry, Geoffrey Taylor, when Poetry Editor of *The Bell* said: "By printing his poems singly, or even in twos and threes, one does not do justice to Mr. O'Sullivan. To get its full and curious flavour his work must be read in larger bulk; so read, his quality comes near to that of John Clare." The bulk of his poetry was published in book form in 1947 (*Lightkeeper's Lyrics*, W. Tempest, Dundalk). He is married and has five children, and contributes both prose and poetry to Irish periodicals.

BLANAID SALKELD (*née* ffrench Mullen) was born in Chittagong, India, (now Pakistan) in 1880 of Irish parents. Returning as a widow to Dublin, where her childhood had been spent, she joined the Gaelic League and got as far as publishing two or three poems in Gaelic, in P. J. Little's *New Ireland*. Contributed to *Aftermath of Easter Week*, a small anthology surreptitiously printed in 1917. Has published occasional translations of Hindustani folk songs, and poems from the Russian, and three volumes of her own poetry. Has also written several verse plays: *Scarecrow Over the Corn* was successfully produced by the Dublin Drama League in 1941. Started the Gayfield Press in 1937 with her artist son Cecil. She lives in Dublin.

EILEEN SHANAHAN (WEBSTER) was born near Dublin in 1901 and was educated at Sion Hill convent and Alexandra College, Dublin. In 1929 she joined the staff of the League of Nations at Geneva; when war came she settled in Surrey, England with her husband and children. She likes the poetry of Francis Ledwidge and F. R. Higgins. Her own poems have appeared in *The Atlantic Monthly*, the *London Mercury*, *The Commonweal* and the *Irish Times*.

WILLIAM BEDELL STANFORD was born in Belfast in 1910, son of a Church of Ireland rector. He received his education at Bishop Foy School, Waterford and Trinity College, Dublin. Became a Fellow of T.C.D. in 1934 and Regius Professor of Greek in 1940. Has written several books on Greek literature and is presently engaged on volume II of his edition of Homer's *Odyssey*.

PATRIC STEVENSON was born at Wadhurst, Sussex in 1909 of Irish parents. Lived in Ireland from the age of ten until he joined the Royal Air Force in September 1940 where he served for five years as radar mechanic. He was educated at Methodist College, Belfast, studied art and specialized in watercolor landscape, has held one-man exhibitions in Dublin, Belfast, Cork, and Waterford. His first book of poems, *Flowing Water*, was published by The Falcon Press, London, in 1946. Since demobilization he has been working as a lecturer in art and music at an adult education centre in England. "My main preoccupation," he writes, "is in giving art lectures and working out new techniques in musical analysis for classes in musical appreciation. . . . I married a violinist, Dorothy Betsy Forster, in 1937 and we have one son, Leslie, born in 1943. Life is overwhelmingly full and far too short."

FRANCIS STUART was born in 1902 in Australia; when he was a few months old his father died and his mother brought him to Ireland. In 1920 he married Maud Gonne's daughter, Iseult; in 1922 he took an active part in the Irish civil war on the Republican side. Before and during World War II he lectured on Irish and English literature at Berlin University and is presently living in the French zone of occupied Germany. His published works include thirteen works of fiction and a book of poems.

GEOFFREY TAYLOR was born in 1900 in Norfolk while his parents were on their way home to Ireland from Australia. He spent his childhood in Sligo and was educated at Trinity College, Dublin, and the Royal College of Science for Ireland. Is interested in natural history and particularly in entomology; did research on the warble fly for the Department of Agriculture, and two books: *Insect Life in Britain* and *Some British Beetles*. Two books of his poems have also been published. *Irish Poets and Poetry of the 19th Century* is shortly to be issued by Routledge.

BRUCE WILLIAMSON was born in 1922, in Belfast. He was educated at Shrewsbury School, England, and at Trinity College, Dublin. He is Literary Editor of the *Irish Times*. In 1944 he collaborated with Greacen and Iremonger in a small volume of verse, *On the Barricades*. His work has appeared in *The Bell* and other periodicals. At the age of 26 he says he hopes to write a couple of novels—and one long poem—about the decline of Anglo-Irish society. He would rather have written Tolstoy's *War and Peace* than Shakespeare's sonnets.

DENIS WRAFTER was born in Ballyduff, Tullamore, in 1910 of farming stock and was educated by the Christian Brothers. He entered the service of the Offaly County Council at 17. He is married, has four children, and farms in his spare time. His poems have appeared in *The Irish Times*, and the *Irish Bookman*.